Driving Successful M&A

Achieving full value from mergers & acquisitions in marketing communications

Critical acclaim for
Driving Successful M&A

A small business guru once said, 'The only reason to start a business is to sell it, and if you don't, you buy it yourself with your blood, sweat and tears.'

The PRCA exists to help members be better businesses. So we welcome this book as it is a helpful guide on how to create business value and then realise it with more certainty.

Crispin Manners
Chairman, Public Relations Consultants Association
and CEO, Kaizo

In a market where there is a relentless cycle of agency consolidation and new start-ups, it's essential that the players are well versed in M&A, and this new publication by Graham Beckett is a valuable contribution from Results.

Hamish Pringle
Director General, Institute of Practitioners in Advertising

M&A in the marketing services sector will always be active, as both clients and agencies recognise the utopia of marrying the scale and depth of services, as well as the economies, of large corporations with the 'fleet of foot' creativity and entrepreneurialism that is the essence of smaller entities. This book provides vital information and guidance on how best to achieve this often elusive goal, and I know it will be welcomed by both parties.

Matthew Hooper
Chairman, Marketing Communications Consultants Association

With the pitifully low success rate of acquisitions closely mirroring that of modern-day marriages, it is little wonder that the M&A process is similarly fraught with risk and full of pitfalls. This book guides the would-be vendor through the M&A jungle step by masterly step, underscoring the necessity to lay the firm foundations and to make the painstaking preparations necessary for success. It also makes it abundantly clear that experienced professional advice is a prerequisite to navigating the many risks and to maximising the rewards. Whilst that is an unsurprising conclusion, in view of the author's pre-eminent position in these matters, it is also self-evidently rock-solid sense, given that most vendors have never experienced the process before.

However, as the timing of a sale is almost always at the behest of the vendor – except in adverse circumstances – the acquirer has to prepare equally carefully, assessing the real reason behind the sale, whether it be a desire for a change in lifestyle, a genuine need for geographical access, a real necessity for critical mass, or simply running out of steam. Having judged accurately why the company is being sold, the buyer then has the critical mission of ensuring that it is the right company, at the right time and at the right price.

All this against a backdrop where the canny buyer wants to buy from a distressed vendor at the bottom of the cycle. And maximum distress is almost always either at the bottom of the cycle or in the early stages of recovery, when the over-indulgence of the good times comes home to roost just as market conditions are at their bleakest or as the first green shoots require working capital to fund growth. Compare the acquisition of AGB by Taylor Nelson (then Addison Consultancy) from the administrators of Maxwell in 1992 to the acquisition by Valin Pollen International (VPI) of The Carter Organization from Don Carter in 1987. The former, judicious acquisition laid the foundations for what is now the world's No. 2 market research company with a market capitalisation of over £1bn, while the latter, imprudent deal drove VPI into administrative liquidation soon after in 1990.

As they say, experience is that which we acquire shortly after we needed it. This book steps in to provide it just in time. It is full of a rare ingredient called common sense which prepares the shrewd vendor to meet the astute buyer in a deal that does not end in the divorce courts or the knacker's yard.

Lorna Tilbian
Director, Numis Securities

Driving Successful M&A

Achieving full value from mergers & acquisitions in marketing communications

Graham Beckett

CEO, Results Business Consulting Ltd, London

PROFILE BOOKS

First published in Great Britain in 2005 by
Profile Books Ltd
58A Hatton Garden
London EC1N 8LX
www.profilebooks.co.uk

A CIP catalogue record for this book is available from the British Library.

ISBN 1 86197 936 3

Designed by Sue Lamble
Typeset in Stone Serif by MacGuru Ltd
info@macguru.org.uk

Printed and bound in Great Britain by Bell & Bain, Glasgow

Contents

About the author

GRAHAM BECKETT started his first marketing and promotional consultancy at the age of 22, selling the business seven years later. He remained with the firm until he joined Golley Slater & Partners in 1981, and within three years he had developed a thriving advertising, PR and marketing services business in London and Dublin, and joined the group board.

He left in 1989, concentrating initially on M&A work in the marketing communications field. He extended this by forming the corporate finance firm, Results Business Consulting, in London, and in 1997 widened the company's interests internationally by establishing Results International. He lives in London and the Cotswolds with his partner, Sharon.

Figures

Foreword

by John Wren, President and CEO, Omnicom Inc., New York

THE MARKETING COMMUNICATIONS INDUSTRY is huge – worth more than $1bn globally – and despite its cyclical nature it continues to grow. It comprises a wide diversity of businesses: advertising agencies; media planning and buying firms; direct marketing agencies and service firms (such as fulfilment houses, call centres and database marketing specialists); sales promotion and events companies; sponsorship/sports/entertainment marketing consultancies; design and PR consultancies; digital and interactive agencies; brand and marketing consultancies; and market research firms. Over the last two decades it has undergone considerable consolidation through merger and acquisition activity. The result has been the emergence of a reduced number of major multinational companies, including Omnicom, of which I am proud to be CEO.

The increased coverage and scale of operation of these businesses have brought particular benefits to three separate stakeholder groups. The first is our clients, who are now offered greater resource and increased stability. They are now able to receive cohesive and coordinated service at a national, international or global level according to their requirements. Staff are the second group to benefit. Increased size allows us to invest centrally in best-of-breed management programmes for our business unit managers and their fast-track emerging stars. Enhanced job opportunity within our various groups goes alongside the training opportunities which scale helps to provide. Lastly, as a result of becoming bigger we are able to provide a continuing and increasing return to our shareholder investors who ultimately finance our growth.

Marketing is vital to the improvement of living standards in the developed and the developing world alike, and marketing communication services make a growing contribution to global GDP. Historically a cottage industry, it is populated by imaginative entrepreneurs whose highly developed craft skills stimulate its ongoing re-invention. Yet together with its increasing importance to client organisations has come the need to institutionalise and consolidate the sector. Today's marketing firms face growing competition for investment in skills, IP and technology developments, in order that they can best meet the changing demands of clients.

As with other dynamic industries, a key ingredient in achieving this goal has been and will continue to be mergers and acquisitions. Omnicom prides itself in having evolved as an acquirer of first choice for high-performance quality marcoms companies, and our sustained record of year-on-year corporate growth is clear evidence of our record of successful M&A process and integration.

Until now, no book has been published which specifically addresses how to create successful mergers and acquisitions in this industry. With this in mind, I believe that this book addresses a highly relevant subject in considerable depth, and I expect that all who read it will gain a wide range of useful insights into a complex, risky, but potentially rewarding aspect of our industry.

John Wren

This book has been produced with the endorsement of the Institute of Practitioners in Advertising (IPA), the Marketing Communications Consultants Association (MCCA), the Public Relations Consultants Association (PRCA) and Numis Securities Ltd, and with contributions from Willott Kingston Smith, Osborne Clark and Lewis Silkin.

1

Introduction

THIS BOOK IS PRIMARILY INTENDED for owners of private marketing communications (or 'marcoms') companies[1] planning the sale of their business, and seeking to ensure that one of the most profound experiences of their life is as successful as possible. It can however also be used by buyers, whose perspective is frequently drawn upon – both to enable independent proprietors to appreciate better the issues that matter to them and in recognition of the fact that even serial buyers often have much to learn about improving the success of their acquisition investments. Throughout the book, the over-riding aim is to support owners in creating over a period of time, and ultimately in realising, the 'sweat equity' in their businesses.

---

1. For the purposes of this book, 'marketing communications' includes advertising agencies, media planning and buying firms, direct marketing agencies and direct marketing services (such as fulfilment, call centres and database marketing), sales promotion, PR, events, sponsorship/sports marketing, design, digital agencies, brand and marketing consultancies, and market research.

It is an unfortunate fact that most research into acquisitions reveals that at least 50 per cent of transactions fail across industry as a whole, at least on the key metric of return on investment (ROI), and often the proportion is nearer to 60 per cent. There is no reason to suppose the position is any better in our own industry. Considerable effort has been expended to determine why this is so, not least by my own company, Results Business Consulting. In 2002, Results sponsored an independent research study carried out by Ashridge Business School into the reasons for this that were, and are, specific to marketing communications companies. The findings were illuminating, if only for demonstrating the inevitable triumph of human fallibility over common sense. That said, there is much for buyers and vendors to learn in this study, and with that in mind I have included an early chapter summarising its findings, and will draw upon it frequently in this book.

at least 50 per cent of transactions fail across industry as a whole, and often the proportion is nearer to 60 per cent

For many owners, putting a business up for sale is an obvious and tempting way of recouping their initial investment, much of which may be measured in blood, sweat and tears. Fortunately there a steady stream of buyers and investors in the industry who are on the lookout for good business properties that have been created by willing and able entrepreneurs. There are a number of client-driven strategic reasons for this; for example, the need to provide a wider range of services or greater geographic cover. Sometimes, of course, sheer naked ambition drives activity.

Perhaps the most powerful motivation comes from investors demanding growth from the publicly traded companies – growth that can't always be achieved organically. This is additionally fuelled by the very strong cash-flow that the industry generally enjoys, notably from media buying, where clients tend to pay in advance of media payment terms requirements. There is relatively little call for capital expenditure in an industry that is largely asset-free, at least in a tangible sense. Consequently, if the cash that is generated were not invested in acquisitions, there would inevitably be calls from shareholders for larger profit distributions.

This book deals mainly with the most common method of releasing value in a private company, that is, a trade sale, and underlines that many of the principles used for building and valuing a business are the same. It does not focus on the other options for releasing value in a private company, such as management buy-out and buy–ins, and 'replacement' and 'development' capital from venture capital firms. Nor does it deal with cross-border transactions (i.e. UK companies acquiring overseas companies), with their myriad additional complications regarding tax, accounting, cultural and business practice differences. My concern here is solely with the acquisition of UK companies, whether by other UK companies or by overseas business entities. Nevertheless, this book should still be instructive for all those involved in M&A activity in the marketing communications industry around the world, as many of the principles detailed here are widely true.

many of the principles used for building and valuing a business are the same

There is one critical piece of advice I would give to all would-be vendors at the outset: whatever you do, be completely open and honest with all your advisers and prospective buyers. Indeed, the book's recommendations and advice are fatally undermined should you choose to do otherwise. Remember: in any people business, it is the character, reputation and above all integrity of individual owners that a buyer is investing in. Be anything other than transparent, and you will seriously jeopardise years of investment in building your business.

Incidentally, on a similar note, signs of individual and corporate modesty are always well received, so if you must indulge in fast cars, boats, planes and women (or men), you will be well advised to keep them out of sight. Needless to say, it is preferable to keep your big, bold moves for the business. Buyers (quite apart from clients and staff) are as prone to adrenaline rushes as the next person. Strong market-driven initiatives that gain real competitive advantage and pricing power can be seen as evidence of firm and inspiring leadership – and that stimulates confidence.

it is the character, reputation and above all integrity of individual owners that a buyer is investing in

Finally, feedback from most vendors after completion of a sale confirms that the process invariably proves to be every bit as traumatic as we at Results told them it would be when we were advising them at the outset. The process, they say, was only made bearable by the fact that they knew what they faced from the start, and were fully supported by trusted, knowledgeable advisers throughout. Having the ability to maintain the necessary momentum of the business throughout the sale process, without major distraction, is one of the most compelling reasons for working with the best advisers available. While I trust that simply reading this book will assist understanding of the sale process and help prospective vendors prepare well for the big day, I also, perhaps unsurprisingly, hope readers will heed this particular piece of advice. Self-serving or not, from time to time in this work I recommend the use of specialist advisers, and I make no apology for doing so.

All references in this book are to the sale of 100 per cent of the shares of a company, other than where expressly stated.

2

Why effective acquisition pays

GIVEN THAT THERE ARE CONSIDERABLE DIFFICULTIES and risks associated with acquisition, why do companies do it? Prominent among a number of reasons is simply ego, which it must be acknowledged has been a key driver for many entrepreneurs over the years. The business world has long played host to individuals who are interested in little short of world domination. To be fair, some great businesses have been created by such people. Yet regretfully some great shareholder value has also been wrecked by people whose need to be big for the sake of bigness has clouded their judgement. Our own industry has not been immune to such examples of hubris. One memorable example in recent times was Cordiant Communications, which finally sold at less than 3p a share, having reached more than £4.10 at one stage.

Fortunately the drivers for growth through acquisition usually have more profound antecedents. These consist primarily of financial and strategic benefits. Financial benefit comes from:

- buying a business at one valuation and later liquidating it at a higher value, for example, by selling it as part of the whole business;

- increasing shareholder value by securing a strong return on the investment (ROI), in much the same way as with any other investment;

- enhancing earnings by aggregating the profits from acquisitions to provide shareholders with a higher level of dividend and, potentially, capital gain return.

Often these activities are somewhat unkindly referred to as 'financial engineering'. This term, however, tends to imply that no real added value is created by the acquirer, other than by simply manipulating assets. Of course this does sometimes happen, but the serious consolidators must add value over time if they are to see sustained benefits, growth and return on investors' capital. If they do not, only relatively short-term, often 'one-off' benefits are gained, and the growth model soon runs out of steam when purchasing power eventually dries up.

serious consolidators must add value over time if they are to see sustained benefits and growth

The need for strategic drivers to acquisition is therefore paramount; that is, where genuine added value results from the 'marriage' of two businesses to create more than a sum-of-the-parts entity. Strategic benefit may take a number of forms – it may bring economic or geographic advantage, new skill sets and disciplines, or management skills and experience. The prospect of client-led benefits, however, is the most persuasive reason for action.

In a fascinating study, Sam Rovit and Catherine Lemire of Bain &

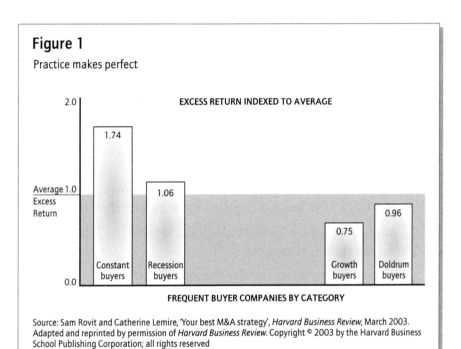

Figure 1

Practice makes perfect

EXCESS RETURN INDEXED TO AVERAGE

2.0

Average 1.0
Excess
Return

0.0

1.74 — Constant buyers

1.06 — Recession buyers

0.75 — Growth buyers

0.96 — Doldrum buyers

FREQUENT BUYER COMPANIES BY CATEGORY

Source: Sam Rovit and Catherine Lemire, 'Your best M&A strategy', *Harvard Business Review*, March 2003. Adapted and reprinted by permission of *Harvard Business Review*. Copyright © 2003 by the Harvard Business School Publishing Corporation; all rights reserved

Company examined 724 acquisitive companies in the USA and the 7,475 acquisitions made by those companies between 1986 and 2001. They then compared the buyers' behaviour pattern with the excess return they made to shareholders in that time (that is, total return to shareholders less the cost of equity).[1]

The simple conclusion Rovit and Lemire reached was that the more deals a company did throughout the economic cycle, the more value it returned to shareholders. The lowest return accrued to those that only made acquisitions during the growth phase.

When Rovit and Lemire looked at the most frequent buyers in more detail, they identified the following common set of disciplines; see Figure 1 on the previous page (and note that 'doldrum' is the stable but uncertain time between recession and growth).

1 Learning vs. feedback: the buyer usually starts with small deals and institutionalises a process based on learning from mistakes.
2 The buyer has a portfolio of identified targets, but is prepared to (and does) walk away from risky deals.
3 Line management are involved at an early stage.
4 There are clear guidelines for integration.

It should be noted that the focus of this study was not on marketing services businesses. However, if we overlay on the results the perennial people issues of most prominence in our industry, the presence of items 3 and 4 from the list above really jumps out.

---

1. 'Your best M&A strategy', Sam Rovit and Catherine Lemire, *Harvard Business Review*, March 2003, p. 16.

3

What makes for effective M&A?

THIS CHAPTER SUMMARISES THE RESEARCH carried out for Results Business Consulting by Ashridge Business School.[1] There were two main reasons for our investment in this study. Firstly, we were keen to establish the real drivers of success in mergers and acquisitions activity in our industry. M&A has a chequered history across all industries as far as delivering shareholder value to buyers (and sometimes to vendors) is concerned – our concern is to ensure that marketing communications outperforms others as the trend towards consolidation becomes a mainstay in the industry.

Secondly, we noted with interest the growing number of risks perceived to have been taken in M&A activity, particularly at the top of the market in the late 1990s. From a purely business perspective, we were anxious to ensure that the deals we were involved in

---

1. Simon Hill, a mature student, carried out the study as part of his MBA at Ashridge in 2002/3.

on behalf of our clients should not have their chances of success jeopardised by these worries.

To summarise the research's main findings,[2] we found that there was scope for greatly improving the execution of M&A. Two key areas were identified: having a clear strategic purpose to a transaction, and strong process excellence. Given the ready availability of academic and prac-titioner-based material on best practice, the results were surprising. Yet despite this, overall deal success rates remain largely unimpres-sive and plenty of shareholder value is eroded. Figure 2 opposite indicates how optimum execution success, as with most business practice, is achieved when both the transac-tional strategy and the process are well thought out. While disasters occur when the opposite happens, even promising strategic deals can be marred by weak process. On the other hand, even poorly conceived transactions can be given a chance of success by strong process.

optimum execution success is achieved when both the strategy and the process are well thought out

In summary, the following issues were identified in these two critical aspects of M&A success:

Transaction strategy

- Holistic due diligence and attention to 'parenting' styles to ensure 'fit'

- Timing of acquisitions, particularly in relation to the economic cycle

---

2. The research involved personal interviews with 6 major UK acquirers and 12 vendors, plus an e-mail questionnaire completed by 31 respondents (from a universe of some 300 transactions in the UK between 1997 and 2002), made up of approximately one-third acquirers and two-thirds vendors.

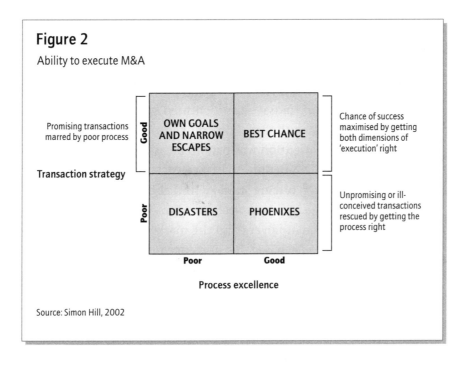

Figure 2

Ability to execute M&A

Promising transactions marred by poor process

Transaction strategy

OWN GOALS AND NARROW ESCAPES

BEST CHANCE

Chance of success maximised by getting both dimensions of 'execution' right

DISASTERS

PHOENIXES

Unpromising or ill-conceived transactions rescued by getting the process right

Good

Poor

Poor   Good

Process excellence

Source: Simon Hill, 2002

- Pursuit of value creation

Process excellence

- Relationship management, including pre-deal clarification of success goals and post-deal communication
- Identifying relevant performance measurement metrics

Transaction strategy

Holistic due diligence

The most successful transactions identified by the research tended to be those on which 'holistic' due diligence had been carried out – that is, detailed attention was paid to areas beyond financial and legal compliance. This definition of 'holistic' includes assessment of the creative product, pricing strategy, and above all the quality and sustainability of the company's relationships with its key audiences – clients, suppliers, employees and the market at large (reputation/ perception). A broader-based due diligence process was also helpful in clarifying the all-important 'fit' criteria.

In particular, the parenting style of the buyer is a useful consideration when assessing relevant fit between acquirer and vendor, and the likelihood of a successful and productive relationship thereafter. Figure 3 shows respondents who subscribe to the belief that all marketing communications, or marcoms, acquirers sit within the fairly complex strategic control 'box' of parenting styles, though some are skewed towards the financial control style.

the parenting style of the buyer is useful when assessing fit between acquirer and vendor

Figure 3

Parenting styles

STRATEGIC PLANNING
- Closely involved with their businesses in the formulation of plans and decisions
- Provides a clear sense of direction
- Large/powerful functional staffs at the centre

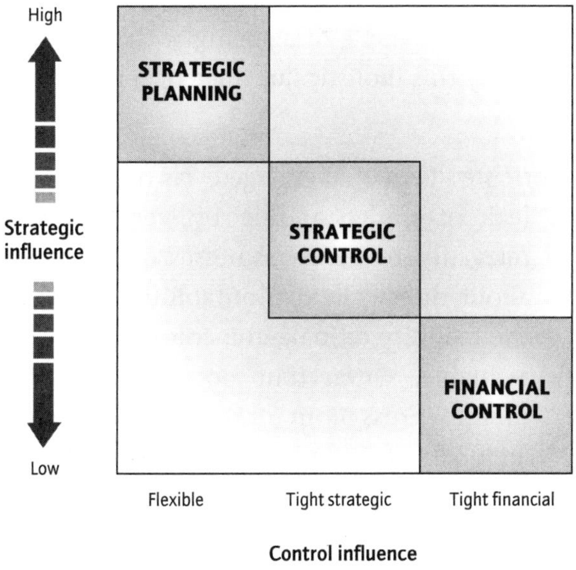

STRATEGIC CONTROL
- Decentralise planning but retain role of checking and assessing business proposals
- Businesses put forward strategies, plans and proposals 'bottom-up' but the parent balances strategic and financial criteria
- Businesses encouraged to work together to achieve synergy benefits but within organisation structures that stress individual business unit performance

FINANCIAL CONTROL
- Strong commitment to decentralised planning
- Structure features standalone business units with maximum autonomy and responsibility for strategies and plans
- Minimum staff at headquarters focused on corporate management support and financial control

High

Strategic influence

Low

STRATEGIC PLANNING

STRATEGIC CONTROL

FINANCIAL CONTROL

Flexible   Tight strategic   Tight financial

Control influence

Source: M. Goold, A. Campbell and M. Alexander, *Corporate-Level Strategy*, John Wiley & Sons, Inc., 1994

The broader relevance of these findings was generally accepted by the key participants, a number of whom expressed interest in how to achieve more robust 'commercial' due diligence, while at the same time seeking a less onerous due diligence process for acquirers. The importance of parenting styles aroused particular interest amongst buyers, with participants keen to position their organisations on the grid, and refresh their understanding of the characteristics of potential vendors most likely to flourish in their own organisations.

As one buyer commented after seeing the research findings:

'I doubt if you'll find many people disagreeing with you on this point. Considered broadly this [holistic due diligence] has to be the way to go.'

A more financially oriented issue that emerged was the widespread lack of understanding by vendors of the relevance to their businesses of information about direct client profitability, and usually the inability to make this information readily available. Often (but not always) vendors monitor gross profit (or revenue) by client, but are unable to set all the company's costs in an equitable manner across the clients in order to understand direct actual client profitability.

the upper quartile of clients creates around 200 per cent of shareholder value

Bain research published in the *Harvard Business Review* in March 2003[3] showed that the upper quartile of clients by profitability in any business typically creates around 200 per cent of shareholder value, while the lower quartile typically destroys the equivalent

---

3. Rovit and Lemire, op. cit.

amount. Thus a company's profits are largely derived from the remaining 50–60 per cent of clients. This finding has a number of important implications:

- Without knowledge of direct (or fully costed) client profitability, agency management is unable to make rational judgements as to the focus of resources, or client compensation negotiations.

- For acquirers, the opportunity to create well-focused synergies to strengthen the acquired company's profitability is severely limited.

- Vendors have the opportunity to maximise value for their property by keeping these measurements in place, quite apart from being able to manage their business more profitably.

Timing of acquisitions

The evidence from the Bain study[4] showed quite clearly that buyers who make transactions consistently throughout the economic cycle gain a much higher shareholder value than those who do not. The contrast is most pronounced with those who follow market sentiment and focus their acquisitions on the upside of the cycle, typically over-paying for weaker properties, and doing so on the basis of less well-honed M&A strategies and processes. The marketing communications industry is no different from other industries in this respect.

What Figure 4 overleaf attempts to show is that the more added value the buyer can bring to the acquired business, the greater

---

4 Ibid.

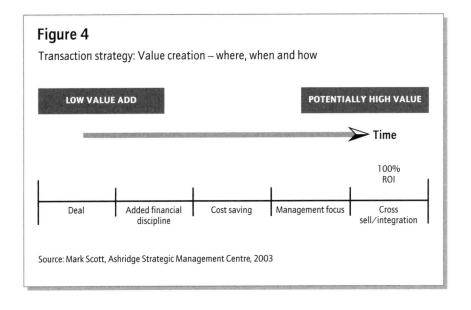

Figure 4

Transaction strategy: Value creation – where, when and how

LOW VALUE ADD   POTENTIALLY HIGH VALUE

Time

100%
ROI

| Deal | Added financial discipline | Cost saving | Management focus | Cross sell/integration |

Source: Mark Scott, Ashridge Strategic Management Centre, 2003

the value creation that is achieved. In marketing communications the focus tends to be limited to the first stage, and efforts to find 'unique' synergies from cross-selling and integration are rare, despite the rhetoric that accompanies most M&A activity. As a result, the question 'How much more is this worth to me than any other acquirer?' does not often get asked, and yet answering it would greatly improve strategic focus, strengthen valuation arguments, and increase accountability for the ROI rationale.

All this is not to overlook the fact that the strictures of earn-out ring-fencing can block synergistic benefits, at least until the earn-out is over. (For more about this, see Chapter 8, on deal structures.) It also provides an explanation as to why acquirers tend to adhere to traditional lagging financial indicators, rather than measure the benefits from investing in management and revenue-led initiatives. Most holding company buyers focus their energies elsewhere, influenced as they are by the short-term demands of capital markets (quarterly reporting, earnings and eps growth) more than by longer-term returns.

Process drivers of M&A success

Relationship management

Most relationships between buyer and vendor display some of the characteristics of a rollercoaster ride right from the outset. Even the initial charm offensive leading up to agreement on a deal can have its stormy moments. Due diligence is often seen as progressively confrontational and things can often get worse during contract negotiations. Eventually collaboration is expected, as the vendor finally becomes part of the buyer's organisation. But the chances

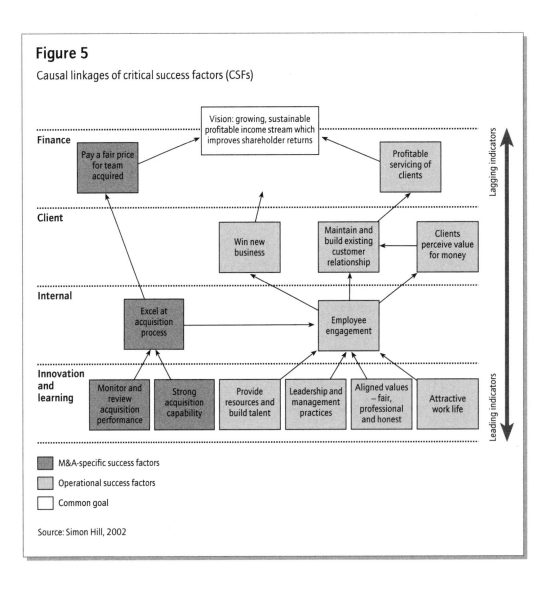

Figure 5

Causal linkages of critical success factors (CSFs)

Finance

Pay a fair price for team acquired

Vision: growing, sustainable profitable income stream which improves shareholder returns

Profitable servicing of clients

Client

Win new business

Maintain and build existing customer relationship

Clients perceive value for money

Internal

Excel at acquisition process

Employee engagement

Innovation and learning

Monitor and review acquisition performance

Strong acquisition capability

Provide resources and build talent

Leadership and management practices

Aligned values – fair, professional and honest

Attractive work life

Lagging indicators

Leading indicators

M&A-specific success factors

Operational success factors

Common goal

Source: Simon Hill, 2002

of this happening can be slim if the buyer is primarily focused on burdensome financial and bureaucratic reporting procedures.

A non-adversarial approach benefits buyers and vendors alike. This can be achieved by establishing a process that uses shared experience to build common objectives. The result is a much better mutual understanding of expectations and value creation. The Ashridge study recommended adoption of 'success maps' along the lines of the hypothetical example below.

a non-adversarial approach benefits buyers and vendors

From a shared understanding of the critical success factors (CSFs) of the normal operational success of a marcoms agency business, it is possible to develop a diagram (see Figure 5 opposite) showing the causal linkages. This can then be developed for the complicating factor of an acquisition. If this exercise is carried out jointly by the acquirer and the vendor, the process can help both parties focus on what is necessary in order to meet the joint objective of a successful transaction.

In essence this provides an opportunity to agree a shared vision of what both parties want to achieve from the deal, and then maps out the likely routes to achieving that. For example, the Ashridge study showed us that there is a substantial body of work to demonstrate how employee engagement leads to strong client satisfaction, which in turn improves and sustains profitability and shareholder value (for which read strong earn-out returns for vendors).

Other key findings on issues of relationship management can be seen in Figure 6 overleaf, which compares vendor and buyer perceptions of process drivers.

The most significant difference of opinion when assessing the best

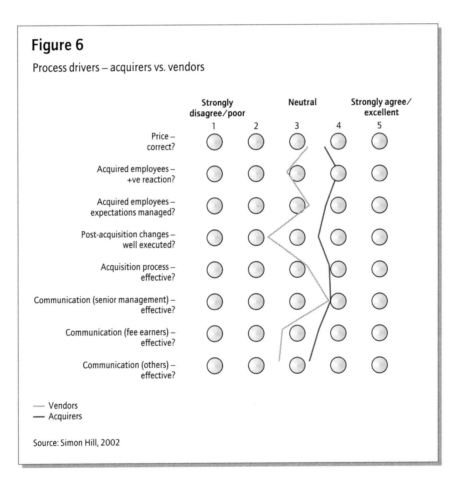

Figure 6

Process drivers – acquirers vs. vendors

	Strongly disagree/poor		Neutral		Strongly agree/excellent
	1	2	3	4	5
Price – correct?	○	○	○	○	○
Acquired employees – +ve reaction?	○	○	○	○	○
Acquired employees – expectations managed?	○	○	○	○	○
Post-acquisition changes – well executed?	○	○	○	○	○
Acquisition process – effective?	○	○	○	○	○
Communication (senior management) – effective?	○	○	○	○	○
Communication (fee earners) – effective?	○	○	○	○	○
Communication (others) – effective?	○	○	○	○	○

—— Vendors
—— Acquirers

Source: Simon Hill, 2002

and worst rated transactions emerged over the implementation of post-acquisition changes. In particular, vendor and acquirer opinion diverged on the issue of employee communication. Although both vendors and buyers felt communication was generally satisfactory at senior management level, vendors felt this was not handled nearly as well for fee earning and other staff (see Figure 6).

There was much anecdotal evidence from the research that neither vendors nor buyers manage communications effectively, but as buyers normally have more experience of the process they should take more responsibility in this area. In addition, the reality is that when vendors tell their senior managers and staff they have sold the business but that nothing will change (or that the future now looks even more exciting), the announcement is usually met with great scepticism. As far as employees are concerned, the psychological employment contract has just been broken and they are now faced with the unknown consequences of having a new employer. The resulting uncertainty about the future can be deeply unsettling, yet is rarely addressed directly and in terms to which the individual can relate.

Given that the research identified a high correlation between the effectiveness of post-acquisition changes (including these critical perceived changes) and transaction success, it is surprising that so little attention is given to a communications strategy for each stakeholder group. The vexation that often occurs over dysfunctional behaviour during earn-outs is therefore no surprise at all.

Performance measurement

Employee and client relationships drive value, yet they are seldom identified and measured, with a few notable exceptions.

As shown in Figure 5 on page 18 it is entirely possible for buyer and vendor to have an early meeting of minds in identifying the critical success factors (CSFs). Accordingly it is possible to discover appropriate key performance indicators (KPIs) and hence measurement processes to ensure that the CSFs are dealt with appropriately. These KPIs should contain a combination of lagging (e.g. financial measures) and leading indicators (e.g. client and employee measures). The advantage of leading measures is the ability to take corrective action before it is too late.

employee and customer relationships drive value, yet they are seldom identified and measured

Figure 7 opposite takes a hypothetical set of understandings reached between a buyer and vendor. Collectively they represent their joint vision for what success would look like and its effect across the business, the critical people issues to be addressed and the KPIs for ensuring that success is achieved, on the basis that 'what you measure is what you get'. The figure clearly indicates that both parties should monitor progress across a range of leading and lagging performance measures, embracing financial, client and employee dimensions.

When these findings were presented to the participant buyers, the central point about using leading performance measures to ensure success was accepted. People quickly became comfortable with the thought process and line of argument. They then wanted to leap to practicalities. What would be the right measures? How would we capture employee and customer data? How frequently would we have to survey people? How do we avoid this becoming perceived as another layer of red tape?

Independent client satisfaction and employee engagement audits are the primary means, but their application needs very careful

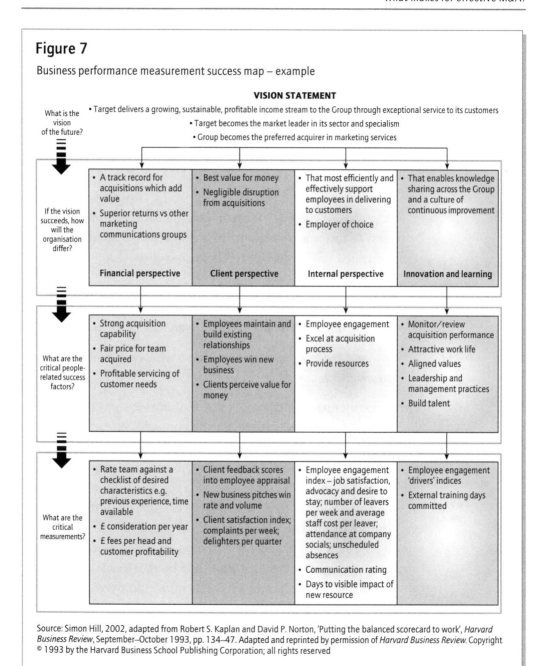

Figure 7

Business performance measurement success map – example

VISION STATEMENT

What is the vision of the future?

- Target delivers a growing, sustainable, profitable income stream to the Group through exceptional service to its customers
- Target becomes the market leader in its sector and specialism
- Group becomes the preferred acquirer in marketing services

If the vision succeeds, how will the organisation differ?

Financial perspective	Client perspective	Internal perspective	Innovation and learning
• A track record for acquisitions which add value • Superior returns vs other marketing communications groups	• Best value for money • Negligible disruption from acquisitions	• That most efficiently and effectively support employees in delivering to customers • Employer of choice	• That enables knowledge sharing across the Group and a culture of continuous improvement

What are the critical people-related success factors?

• Strong acquisition capability • Fair price for team acquired • Profitable servicing of customer needs	• Employees maintain and build existing relationships • Employees win new business • Clients perceive value for money	• Employee engagement • Excel at acquisition process • Provide resources	• Monitor/review acquisition performance • Attractive work life • Aligned values • Leadership and management practices • Build talent

What are the critical measurements?

• Rate team against a checklist of desired characteristics e.g. previous experience, time available • £ consideration per year • £ fees per head and customer profitability	• Client feedback scores into employee appraisal • New business pitches win rate and volume • Client satisfaction index; complaints per week; delighters per quarter	• Employee engagement index – job satisfaction, advocacy and desire to stay; number of leavers per week and average staff cost per leaver; attendance at company socials; unscheduled absences • Communication rating • Days to visible impact of new resource	• Employee engagement 'drivers' indices • External training days committed

Source: Simon Hill, 2002, adapted from Robert S. Kaplan and David P. Norton, 'Putting the balanced scorecard to work', *Harvard Business Review*, September–October 1993, pp. 134–47. Adapted and reprinted by permission of *Harvard Business Review*. Copyright © 1993 by the Harvard Business School Publishing Corporation; all rights reserved

management to safeguard the relationship between the new parent and subsidiary (the suspicion of 'big brother' interference is one obvious potential risk). Ideally these measurement tools would be in place before the sale process, which would clearly add value to the vendor's business.

Some interesting comments were received regarding this critical area of the conclusions:

> 'The process of building the causal linkages between critical success factors would be really useful if undertaken up front by acquirer and vendor working together.'

> 'The four factors you've pinpointed as driving employee engagement are precisely my main focus at present. Ways for measuring and hence managing these would be really useful.'

> 'We would expect acquisition targets to have client satisfaction measurement processes in place.'

A further conclusion of the study was that buyers should be encouraged not only to consider aligning earn-out payments with financial performance, but to embrace these other indicators too, given their impact on value creation. Developing the earn-out model to incorporate measurement of customer and employee satisfaction would provide a mechanism to protect acquirers from margin erosion, or even implosion, in the post earn-out period. Employee and client satisfaction data would become common currency of management reporting throughout the earn-out. And by part-gearing the applicable multiple to the levels of client and employee satisfaction achieved, vendors could be presented with a powerful incentive.

This concept aroused much debate and interest amongst buyers, and we may well see its application in the comparatively near future. As one buyer said, 'The concept of enhancing earn-outs where high levels of employee and client measures are achieved is particularly exciting.'

The level of interest and participation in this study by buyers and vendors was high and it is clear that attitudes have been influenced by the work carried out by Simon Hill. This work will undoubtedly shape much-needed improvements in the quality of returns to both buyers and vendors from acquisition activity.

The findings of the Ashridge research correspond on the whole to my experience, but I would like to add one important point of my own. It is, in my view, relevant to understand the negotiation environment and style of the buyer. Specifically there is a great difference between those organisations in which the negotiators and their process are focused solely on completing the deal, with no personal commitment or accountability to the long-term outcome, and those where the opposite is true.

The negotiation process and its likely outcome will be totally different in each set of circumstances. When the people involved view the eventual contracted agreement as the start rather than the end of the process, they will be motivated to ensure that both parties are committed to working together to create meaningful added value. But when a deal is being done simply because a deal *must* be done, negotiation is characterised by a 'no prisoners' mentality in which the negotiator relentlessly seeks advantage over the vendor. Typically this involves over-promising, moving the goalposts (usually very late in the day), and almost certainly regarding the due diligence process as a means to change what has previously been agreed. Artificial deadlines, apparent loss of interest and other intimidation tactics will usually be used to 'soften up' the vendor.

Much energy also goes into manufacturing onerous warranties and penalty clauses.

Whilst this may appear to be an utterly pointless approach – and fortunately it is the exception rather than the rule – it does nevertheless still occur in varying degrees. When it is encountered, it should be taken as a real warning to vendors who will normally and quite rightly be relying on the implementation of the deal, rather than the deal itself, to fulfil their value expectations over the earn-out period and beyond. An adviser with intimate understanding of all the available buyers, and their respective approaches to negotiation, will be invaluable in understanding these risks.

Finally I should also point out that the deal-orientated approach is not exclusively the domain of certain buyers. Greed and avarice have been known to overcome vendors also, who can become blinded by short-term gain. Serious buyers, however, can recognise such people a mile off, and will normally give them a wide berth – and when they don't, they always live to regret it.

Either way, I strongly believe that if simply signing the deal is the only goal in mind for either the buyer or the vendor (or both), then a winning deal for both parties will not materialise. When it is recognised that winning is the result not of signing a contract but of real work by both parties over time, then great value can be created.

4

Why people sell

AT THE RISK OF STATING THE OBVIOUS, people sell primarily to capitalise on the otherwise illiquid asset represented by their shareholding in a proprietorial business. Often the business is one they founded themselves, with or without partners. If the reason for a sale is reasonably straightforward, its timing bears greater investigation. The rationale for a planned exit will vary, but it may be for retirement purposes (including well before normal retirement age in some cases), or in order to gain early family security, or to secure a step-change strategically in the scale and/or direction of the firm or the career of the principals. Other reasons might include the need to remove at an early stage a shareholder who is not involved in the business (an investor, a retiree, a non-performer or the victim of ill health), or indeed even to resolve a divorce settlement.

All of this may be accelerated by the existence of an unsolicited attractive offer, which a quality firm will almost certainly attract as it matures and begins to make its presence known in the market. This can of course prove to be a good time to sell, if all the premium factors described in Chapter 9 are in place. If they are not, then the timing is probably wrong.

even if the timing feels right, it is risky to enter into negotiations without professional support

Yet even if the timing feels right, it is risky to enter into exclusive negotiations with any predator without engaging full professional advisory support (and being seen to do so), and without treating the situation just as you would if you were taking a proactive approach to marketing the business for sale.

Presenting the business in its best light and seeking competitive bids will always make sense. Without this approach you have no way of knowing that the predator's approach is the best one available for you. Bear in mind that you will not normally have another chance of getting it right.

All that having been said, it is quite legitimate to make a sale for personal reasons, such as impending retirement or simply a desire to secure family finances. However, as always, there are different ways of dealing with these requirements; choosing the right way makes the difference between a successful and an unsuccessful sale, although whatever happens, up-front honesty about intentions is always required.

In the case of retirement, the key issue is when to sell in relation to the proposed retirement age. Given that it is normal for the shareholders of a marcoms business to enter into an earn-out agreement, a period of up to five years must be allowed for up to the retirement date. It should be noted, however, that there tends to be less interest in vendors who are much over 50, particularly with smaller companies. This is because of the perception that the industry is a young person's 'game' and that principals will be losing ambition and drive for continued growth once they are into their 50s. Clearly there are many people of this age who regard themselves as having many more miles left on the clock, but we are dealing here with perceptions, and the fact is that generally speaking vendors in their 50s are perceived as a less attractive proposition.

Any buyer needs to be convinced that there are good people in the business who can eventually take over the baton from the owners, but clearly this requirement is especially critical where vendors are potentially near to retirement, or have specifically stated their retirement intentions.

As for the desire to primarily secure family finances – this can work fine, provided that the buyer is not left wondering whether the vendor is also intending to wind down their involvement with the business, in which case the preceding comments concerning retirement apply. Clearly if this is actually the intention, and the vendor is prepared for the trade-off in terms of value and is honest about this, then there is no particular problem – subject once again to reassurance that there are good people who can take over the management in due course.

What most buyers would like to hear, provided it is absolutely true, of course, is that the primary reason for selling is to enhance professional career prospects for the vendors and their employees. Buyers are likely to respond favourably to a very real vision of how this can be achieved through a strategic business partnership. This will be a particularly credible proposition to a buyer after the business has already established a sound market reputation and a good performance record. Companies in this position are those to which buyers are most readily attracted; where there is strong evidence of the probability of continued growth as part of the buyer's environment, and an expectation that the principals will wish to continue with the buyer's organisation well beyond the earn-out conclusion.

There are other times to consider a sale or merger during the earlier stages of a business life cycle. For example, the principals may realise they can grow much more quickly by coming together with one or more other companies who may provide economic and strategic means of fast-tracking the business life-cycle. These may be businesses with complementary or even the same clients, skill sets or technology that will create a stronger, more competitive position. Carefully thought-through transactions of this nature represent evolutionary steps towards creating a more valuable eventual sale to a major company. They will make a lot of sense if the principals in a proposed merger know they can get on well and can reconcile themselves to a fair and equitable share in the combined new venture, and can resolve all the attendant issues over cultural and commercial compatibility and management control.

These things are not always easy, however, in an industry that is often unfortunately plagued by egos. Culture differences are also often overlooked, with no two businesses ever likely to share the same DNA. It is therefore important first to recognise the differences, and then to look for a new culture that both parties are prepared to embrace in order to occupy common ground.

It is also important to understand that such 'mergers' should ideally take place at least a couple of years before a sale of the combined entity is planned. This is because a buyer will be suspicious of the success of such transactions, especially where they have involved physical mergers. In such circumstances there is a real need to feel that sufficient time has passed to prove the success of the deal, before embarking on a further transaction.

5

Timing and the economic cycle

WHEN PLANNING A SALE, timing is important in many different areas, including the age of the principals or the age and maturity of the business, as discussed in the previous chapter. The economic cycle must also be considered, and the general assumption here is that selling at the top of the market is best, while selling at the bottom is ill advised. Like many assumptions, there is some truth in this, but the reality is not necessarily that clear cut.

There is an old joke about an Englishman who gets lost in rural Ireland. When he stops to ask a local for directions to his destination, the local replies, 'Well, I wouldn't start from here.' More than a few private company vendors who sold during the last market peak in 2000 may be feeling rather like that now.

One of the must-dos about earn-outs, and the basis for the vast majority of private company sales in the sector, is – get off to a good start. Vendors are commonly advised that the strongest underpinning for any deal negotiation is to report continuing rising results during the period of talks with buyers. But those who sold on figures from

2000 and whose 2001 results were consistently ahead of the previous year's were firmly in the minority. For some, it may well have been that their whole earn-out was blighted by the events of 2001.

So, curiously, those who didn't ride the tide of mergers and acquisitions in 2000/1 may not have missed the boat in the way that some believed. If 2002 or 2003 were taken as the base year for the calculation of the value of their business, even if results were down only slightly, it may be that an earn-out based on either of those years will yield more over its term than a 2000 deal, despite there being a smaller up-front payment.

one of the must-dos about earn-outs is – get off to a good start

Consider the following scenario, as illustrated in Figure 8. Good 2000, buoyant prospects; set-back in 2001 as spends fall over; respectable 'bounce' and good growth through 2002–4:

Now consider a simple deal structure, in which the consideration paid is calculated as follows:

- 5 times pre-tax profit (£400,000) at closing;

- 5 times average pre-tax profits over 3 years (including the base year), rising to 6 if growth equals or exceeds 20 per cent.

- If your deal started on the base year 2000, the effect of the poor 2001 result is that the deal will never yield any earn-out and will therefore total the £2m up front (£400,000 times the multiple) alone.

- For a deal starting in 2001, however, while the up front will fall significantly to £1.5m, the earn-out will blossom to a total of £1m (6 × £416k, less the initial £1.5m payment). This gives total consideration of £2.5m, a significant increase on the 2000-based deal.

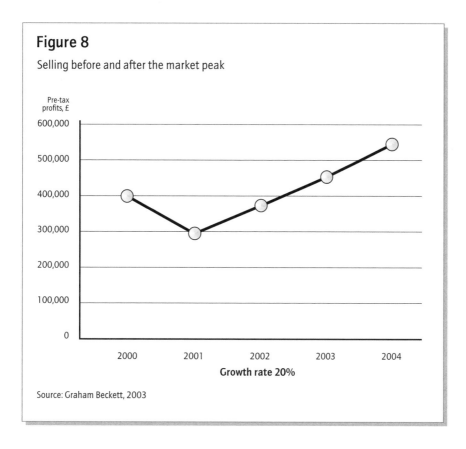

Figure 8

Selling before and after the market peak

Pre-tax profits, £

Growth rate 20%

Source: Graham Beckett, 2003

Admittedly the delayed receipt of the money reduces the net present value of the deal. There is also an inevitable degree of uncertainty during the earn-out (although it is worth pointing out that the smooth growth shown here is not necessary: only a 20+ per cent growth from the base year to the final year and average profits at a comparable level over the earnout period are required). But on the plus side, there is a real prospect of getting off to a good start, a key feature of successful deals as noted above, followed by three years of upside, continually boosting the payout. Quite a contrast to the drudgery of spending that time bemoaning the impossibility of increasing the total amount you will get.

The permutations are, of course, endless. But what this shows is that selling after the market peak does not necessarily mean missing the boat. You may even be pleased you didn't take the proffered shilling (or millions thereof) from one of the big players, as you could be better off selling just as the market starts to rise again, given the relative certainty of growth over the life of the earn-out. You would have the prospect of a positive and successful earn-out with an icing-on-the-cake final payment, and have avoided three years or more staring at a glass of flat champagne. And if, as is common, a proportion of the consideration had been taken in high priced stock, the real value of the deal could prove to have been very much lower than the initial valuation.

selling after the market peak does not necessarily mean missing the boat

There will, of course, be optimum points in the cycle when it is best to sell, but judging exactly when they are is very difficult without the benefit of hindsight. A decision to sell somewhere near midway up the cycle, perhaps two to three years after recovery, would seem to represent the best time. In that event the number of prospective buyers, and therefore bidding competition, would be near peak, and there would remain at least three good growth years ahead to maximise the earn-out. All the same, preparing the business for sale to meet such a timescale is inevitably a challenge.

Conversely, even when there are relatively few buyers in the market at the bottom of the cycle, it is probably not fruitful to sell a good property at this time. Outside this period, though, our experience is that there is almost always a market for a really good business, and strong premium qualities always generate interest.

At the top of a market boom, at times of frothy asset values, it is true that valuations can get absurdly unrealistic. Bust always follows boom, however, and as we have illustrated here, the consequences for a vendor relying on an earn-out can be quite miserable. Apart from aberrations such as the late 1990s dotcom bubble, market valuations vary over time far less than one might think, for the very simple reason that the laws of arithmetic (and of return on investment) don't change.

there is almost always a market for a really good business

Overall, the key issue is to aim to get the timing right for the maturity and growth of the business (and these are linked to the issues of the vendor's age and succession management, as mentioned in the previous chapter). We normally use the conventional growth curve graph to explain this to prospective vendors (see Figure 9 overleaf). Buyers tend to view the business life cycle in simplistic terms. It is, as a generalisation, not an attractive proposition to sell a business less than three years old, with profits yet to rise much over a few hundred thousand pounds, and a relatively unproven track record.

There is a natural tendency to believe that a great time to sell is at the top of the business life cycle, when profits are being maximised

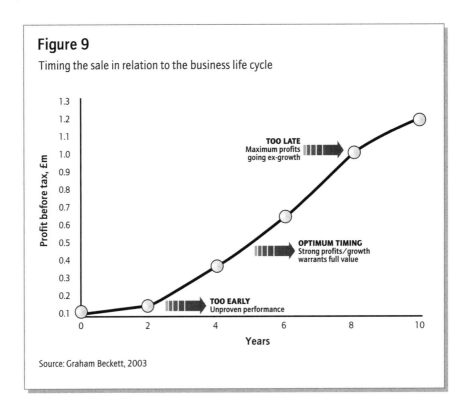

Figure 9

Timing the sale in relation to the business life cycle

Source: Graham Beckett, 2003

and a prospectively high multiple will provide stratospheric returns. Unfortunately, the astute buyer has been here before and will quickly spot that the business may be about to reach the point where growth is about to expire, particularly where it is obvious that the business has been 'ramped'. This means that the principals have deliberately under-invested in talent, management, technology, property, client service, and so on, to minimise costs and maximise short-term profits.

Understandably, a business going ex-growth in this way, or at least perceived to be so doing, will not command a high multiple – indeed it will almost certainly be discounted, regardless of the size of profits. This discounting is in order to reflect the risk of not getting a decent return on the investment, which, as with any other kind of investment, can normally only come from growth.

By contrast, a decision to sell midway through the business growth curve is likely to provide the optimum circumstances for a premium priced deal. Here, the buyer can be reassured by a good track record of consistent profitability and growth and evidence that there is a sound growth strategy in place. The following simplified hypothetical example indicates how much better off a vendor is in this scenario – even without the benefit of the three years of extra cash generated that the earlier deal provides, and the resultant earlier retirement from the business (where that is an issue for the vendor).

Selling at top of company's life cycle

- Pre-tax profits of £900,000, at a multiple of 6 = initial value of £5.4m; assume (typically) 60 per cent paid up front (= £3.2m), and balance to be built into earn-out.

■ Earn-out based on multiple of 6 for average profit growth of 10+ per cent over three years = zero payout.

■ Total consideration: £3.2m.

Selling at mid-cycle

■ Pre-tax profits of £600,000, at a multiple of 6.5 = initial valuation of £3.9m; assume 60 per cent paid up front (= £2.34m), and balance to be built into earn-out.

■ Earn-out based on multiple of 6.5 for average growth of 10+ per cent over three years: £900k × 6.5 = £5.85m, less initial consideration of £3.51m.

■ Total consideration: £5.85m.

A fairly conclusive case.

6

Managing the process

ONE OF THE BIGGEST STUMBLING BLOCKS to a successful conclusion
of a private company sale is the understandable lack of experience
of the majority of vendors, and the consequent gulf in communications between the buyer and the vendor. What may appear normal
market practice to the acquirer can seem unfamiliar and unacceptable to the prospective
vendor. He may find a buyer's requests for
information excessive, the negotiation tactics
aggressive, due diligence laborious, and the
terms and conditions onerous. The vendor's
reaction to all this may seem irrational to those
with whom he is dealing. Moreover, his limited knowledge of M&A
and financial markets may leave him with unrealistic expectations
of the value of his company. There is therefore a real danger that one
or both sides may increasingly come to feel that the other is being
unreasonable, until the point is reached where talks collapse.

one of the biggest
stumbling blocks is the
lack of experience of
the majority of vendors

Accordingly, the chances of a successful conclusion can be significantly enhanced if a prospective vendor is well briefed as to what to expect from the disposal process, both in terms of its various stages and in terms of market conditions.

It would not be unusual for a shareholder in a privately owned company to have very little appreciation of the time and effort that goes into a company sale. In many such companies the owners are the managers and, except in the case of larger enterprises, the management team is small and there are no outside directors. Running such a business is a full-time process for management and so the additional workload that is involved in selling is significant. It will probably involve providing copious information, lengthy negotiation meetings with one or several parties, and dealing with lawyers, accountants and other advisers on both sides. All these activities create a burden that can weigh heavily on the day-to-day running of the company. Additionally, both the fact of selling one's own company and the process itself are stressful and emotionally draining.

The temptation is for the owner to become absorbed by the process to the detriment of his business – and at the worst time, too. Clients, contracts and key personnel are easily lost when one's eye is off the ball.

Meticulous time-planning and preparation are therefore essential if management is to handle everything effectively. Delegation, though not always a developed art in such companies, is an important aspect of this. The enlightened manager will nevertheless focus on driving the performance of the business and allow advisers to take responsibility for the selling process, whilst being available at all key moments.

We occasionally come across owners who are reluctant to take a proactive approach to selling their business for fear of being seen as weak in their negotiating position. They prefer to wait until predators approach them – even though they would hardly be likely to try a similar tack if they wanted to sell their car or home. Actually, it is very hard to understand this sensitivity. Waiting until an approach is received is almost certainly a sure-fire way of *not* securing the best value or of experiencing an exhausting and time-consuming failed transaction. We know of agency entrepreneurs who regularly entertain approaches, but who serially fail to complete a deal. In most cases they missed the best price they could have got for their business. And while they spend inordinate amounts of time on abortive deals, they create a reputation for themselves that makes them progressively less attractive to prospective buyers.

waiting until an approach is received is a sure-fire way of not securing the best value

The reasons why the passive approach usually fails to deliver full value are clear. Firstly, the vendor is not in control of the process right from the start, which they must be if they are ever to have a chance of securing what they want, and even of understanding what their expectations realistically should be. The approach will have been made on timing to suit the acquirer, who will probably have done their homework and have far more knowledge of the vendor than the other way round. The second reason is that the vendor will inevitably be flattered and seduced by the approach. This means they will have no process of their own or any competitive pressure to bring to bear that will encourage the buyer to do otherwise than set the value parameters and the timescale to their own advantage. Above all, without a competitive offer in the frame, the psychological leverage to negotiation does not exist and the vendor never knows whether or not they have secured the best price or strategy from the market.

Nor should it be overlooked that this process ignores the fact that the buyer may well not be the best partner available for the vendor. This is extremely important, as the Ashridge research emphasised. Given that a significant proportion of the consideration will normally be a performance-related, deferred or earn-out payment, it is critical that the buyer finds themselves in the embrace of an organisation in which they will flourish. Hence issues over selection of compatible cultures and strategic significance are critical for both parties. It is therefore dangerous to agree a deal without having had equally intimate dialogue with a select number of relevant potential partners.

it is critical that the buyer finds themselves in the embrace of an organisation in which they will flourish

Starting the process; grooming the business for sale

By 'process' here I am referring to the whole exercise, from starting the exit planning (by which I mean sale, not departure from the business) through to the final consideration received for the sale of the owner's shares. This can take many years. Working backwards, the earn-out, which will be the normal requirement, can take up to five years; while the sale process, from starting the Information Memorandum preparation through to contract completion (and receipt of the initial payment), will probably take up to a year. In addition, before this the exit planning and pre-sale preparation must have been firmly in place for at least three years.

The process should actually start when the business is formed. When Results is involved in working with start-up teams, we strongly encourage these entrepreneurs to look forward to the 'big day' from the outset. This very much helps concentrate the mind as to how the business should appear to an eventual buyer, and enables plans for imbuing it from the outset with the kind of premium values that will ultimately achieve maximum value. This can start with formulating the correct shareholding structure, shareholder's agreement and Articles of Association from an eventual sale perspective.

When we start work with owners on their exit strategy, we scrutinise the business from the point of view of a prospective investor. This means that it is forensically examined as it would be in a due diligence exercise, and a complete commercial perspective is taken using benchmarked competitive data. The result is a platform of critical understanding about where the business stands in relation to its peers, and the value goals the owners have for the business. This in turn helps set out a road-map of actions to be taken over time to reach the desired position. The road-map provides an immensely useful reference tool for all key decisions and judgements about the business from that point forward.

Above and beyond anything else, a company should endeavour to clean up its affairs well before a sale is under consideration. Basically it must adopt the type of professional management procedures that are expected of any established, probably public, buyer. This aside, a predatory approach may be received at any stage, for which it is obviously best to be well prepared. Items and actions on the agenda for attention should include:

- Up-to-date and well-prepared financial management information, made available on a monthly basis. A buyer will always base a view on the confidence they have in the company's financial director, which in turn will significantly affect overall value. If, for example, the FD, regardless of competence, is clearly little more than a yes-man for the owners, he will inspire little confidence.

- Business planning and track record: a history of accurate planning and forecasting represents an ideal platform for a buyer to trust the projections set out in the Information Memorandum. However, this is not often a strong point in private companies. If time permits, it is worth starting this process immediately, in order to generate a credible track record and also as a rehearsal for preparing the actual Information Memorandum.

- Accounting policies should be reviewed so that they will not come under attack for overstating the performance of the business. Work in progress and depreciation policies, for example, should be managed on as prudent a basis as possible.

- Ensure positive cash flow is achieved. Often poor cash flow is a function of weak collection of receivables (debtors), resulting in unnecessary and costly use of borrowing facilities. Receivables beyond 90 days also tend to become much harder to collect; indeed, buyers tend to assume these are to be written off, and value is reduced accordingly.

- Always ensure that VAT (sales tax) and PAYE (employment taxes and social insurance costs) returns are up to date and any queries are dealt with promptly and efficiently.

- All staff should have proper contracts of employment, and senior executives responsible for the company's clients and 'product' must have realistic service agreements to provide proper protection for the company's trade.

- Slack treatment of 'freelancers' must be eradicated in order to avoid the risk of the company being found liable for these people's tax and NIC liabilities.
- Client contracts should be secured and signed. Profits should not be made outside the terms of the client contracts, such as mark-ups or commissions contrary to the agreement.
- Lease agreements should be readily available and any onerous long-term arrangements avoided.
- Shareholder agreements should be in place.
- Maintenance of a fixed asset schedule is advised.
- The company's systems, IT and controls must be regularly reviewed and competitively up to date.

This is not intended to be an exhaustive list, but simply one that is indicative of a well-run company in the normal course of business.

Valuation

About 12–18 months from the outset of the sale process, it is advisable to have the business formally valued to verify value expectations before proceeding. Chapter 9 shows that valuation is far from an exact science; however, provided the valuer has first-hand, specialist knowledge of the contemporary marketplace there are unlikely to be any nasty surprises. Most valuers will err on the side of conservatism in their estimation, in any case.

Appointing advisers

Once it is apparent that the path is cleared for the opening stages, you must finalise your team of advisers. Lord Hanson, who was an experienced acquirer, listed this as one of his 'musts' for successful acquisition. According to him, you should 'ensure that you have assembled the best possible team of advisers. Lawyers, merchant bankers, brokers, consultants and PR advisers can make or break a significant deal.' Buyers, of course, may be involved in a number of transactions. A vendor, on the other hand, usually only gets one chance to sell their business – that's one chance to get it right. In most cases it is their largest personal asset, and the level of personal loss should they not maximise their return is very high. Lord Hanson's advice is probably therefore twice as relevant for a vendor.

> a vendor usually only gets one chance to sell their business – one chance to get it right

How then do you ensure you are represented by the best professional corporate finance, accounting, tax and legal advisers in the market? Well, it is preferable that they have first-hand experience of working with the prospective buyers in the sector. This will save a substantial amount of time, if nothing else. Knowledge of how particular buyers operate and think about their business, create their deal structure, and manage the due diligence and legal process, is invaluable.

The most effective way to identify high-quality advisers, however, is by seeking advice from other vendors you are aware of, and from trade bodies, such as the Institute of Practitioners in Advertising (IPA), Direct Marketing Association (DMA) and Public Relations Consultants Association (PRCA), who represent marketing communications businesses in the UK. If appropriate, issue a very clear brief of what services you expect from such advisers and request a formal proposal which is unequivocal about fees, terms and conditions, the services to be supplied, and what is in return expected from the client.

Agreeing the adviser's terms of engagement and fees

For both client and adviser, it is essential to specify precisely the objective to be achieved and the responsibilities to be assumed by the adviser. Fees should be set out clearly, otherwise this can be a matter for disagreement between client and adviser at the end of the process.

Usually the fee structure for your corporate finance adviser will include a time-based fee from the outset. This establishes a commitment to a successful outcome on the part of both vendor and adviser, and is often deducted from any success fees that fall due. A success fee is usually based on a percentage of the deal value.

An adviser will often want to protect their position. There are a number of ways they can do so, for example by:

- Providing for an exclusive representation, such that a success fee is payable even if they were not responsible for introducing the eventual buyer. This prevents offers secured by the adviser being used by the vendor to establish a price for a party whom the vendor has privately ascertained is ready to buy.

- Defining deal value with great care, so that it is clear how the success fee is to be calculated. Deal value will generally be defined as the aggregate of the price paid for the shares that are sold, whether in the form of equity, quasi-equity or debt (including any deferred consideration), plus the value of any external financial debt responsibility taken on by the acquirer (including all amounts due to shareholders and overdrafts, less cash balances), together with the value of any non-cash consideration and any other consideration payable to dividends and remuneration in excess of normal rates.

- Providing for an 'abort' fee to be paid when the adviser has brought in one or more offers, on which the vendor declines to proceed for whatever reason.

The lead adviser's role

The corporate finance adviser, as the lead adviser, will adopt a coordination role, assuming responsibility for the execution of the sale process while working closely with their principal. The adviser will additionally carry out a number of other functions, notably:

- Assisting the creation of a short-list of candidates, and making discreet approaches.
- Preparing an appropriate 'no-name' summary for use in initial approaches, drafting an Information Memorandum and producing a confidentiality agreement.
- Advising as to negotiation strategy, tactics and general approach.
- Acting to defuse personal tension between principals by taking on responsibility for negotiating key matters of friction.
- Proposing deal structures that will enhance the outcome for the prospective vendor.
- Advising his principal as to whether the price and terms of received offers are acceptable under current market circumstances.

The lead adviser is likely to work with other advisers who are brought into the team at appropriate phases of progress. These will include lawyers, auditors, accounting and tax advisers.

In the case of a privately owned company sale, effective client management by the adviser is not necessarily for the faint-hearted. For a prospective vendor who faces for the first time the prospect of selling a cherished company, and who is unfamiliar with the process, the experience is both personal and stressful. The adviser has therefore to make great efforts to ensure that the process is conducted in a professional way and is not upset by erratic behaviour, unreasonable demands, jumping the gun or emotional responses to negotiations. The unaccustomed pressure of difficult negotiations can often lead to a major 'wobble' by the vendor. At times like these, the adviser can be left fighting fires just to try to keep the deal together.

the prospect of selling a cherished company is both personal and stressful

Preparation for marketing

Once you have appointed your 'team', the corporate finance advisers are the first 'on stage'. They must start by carrying out whatever review of the business and the market is necessary to satisfy both themselves and the client that they can achieve a sale at or above the expected valuation. If the adviser is the same as that responsible for the original valuation, then, unless there have been any radical changes, there will probably be relatively little work involved at this stage, provided the evaluation work was carried out less than a couple of years before the sale process gets under way.

The advisers will then start work on a draft Information Memorandum, setting out sufficient and concise disclosure for prospective buyers to base their offers on. That aside, this document is naturally very much a selling document. It helps focus the buyer on, among other things, a clear understanding of the background and competitive positioning of the business, its performance and growth prospects, key client and employee information.

The process of preparing this document also serves to get all involved on 'the same page' in terms of exactly how the business is to be presented strategically to maximise value. This in turn stimulates discussion of which buyer selection criteria are to be used. Generally, this discussion should encompass the cultural and commercial 'fit' sought, client alignments, deal structure preferences, strategic benefits, and so on. Once agreement in this area is reached, it will help the advisers convert their research into an initial long list of prospective buyers. These are then reviewed in detail with the client against the agreed criteria in order to arrive at a short-list of relevant candidates.

Confidentiality

This is always a concern when a company is to be sold, and possible breaches of confidentiality should be a major preoccupation. The first area of concern centres on the fact that, should the owner's willingness to sell become known, it could destabilise a close-knit team of employees, affect relations with clients and suppliers, and generate unhelpful rumours in the marketplace. Secondly, there is concern as to the misuse of the sensitive commercial information provided in order to allow interested parties to evaluate the company.

Experience suggests that prospective acquirers do take confidentiality agreements seriously and a well-drafted non-disclosure agreement (NDA) document to this effect should be agreed before any sensitive information is provided. Nevertheless, there are steps that can be taken to further reduce risk. These include:

- Using an adviser to make initial approaches on the basis of a 'blind' company profile that prevents easy identification of the target.

- Initially, restricting to a minimum the provision of information that allows an indicative offer to be made. It is our general practice at Results to limit distribution of Information Memoranda to those buyers with whom good personal chemistry has been established and where definite interest to make an offer has been expressed.

- Conducting negotiations away from the target company, such as at the adviser's premises, and refusing to allow interested parties to visit or contact the vendor's employees until permission is granted. Such permission will normally be granted, at the earliest, only when an acceptable indicative offer is received.

- Withholding the most sensitive information, such as named customer details, until a late stage in the discussions, when a deal looks close.

- Maintaining momentum so that the timetable is as short as possible.

The risk can never be completely eliminated, however, and it is therefore as well to have contingency plans for dealing with a leak in case one should actually occur.

Starting the marketing

Most corporate finance advisers – generalists in particular – then make contact with the names on the short-list (indeed, many go to all those on a long-list). Wherever interest is forthcoming, an NDA will be obtained and the Information Memorandum mailed to the buyer.

At Results, our own approach is quite different. We feel that vendors should not subject themselves to such unqualified exposure in the marketplace, as, quite apart from unnecessary disclosure about their business, it leads to much wasted effort and false expectations. Regardless of the existence of confidentiality agreements, the fragile nature of these businesses should be put at no more risk than is absolutely necessary.

Our strong preference is to 'interview' the prospective buyer, without revealing the identity of the client, with the intention of verifying our knowledge and research, and the suitability of the buyer measured against the agreed selection criteria. We probe all the relevant issues of their ambitions and prior success in the space we are dealing with, the reporting lines likely to be involved, the relationship to their strategic priorities, and generally seek to understand the strength of their 'need' as opposed to 'nice to have' intentions. To assist the process we prepare a one-page synopsis of the business as a Preliminary Sale Advice notice. This provides the prospective buyer with a clear statement of the proposition, positioning, background and financial dynamics. In other words, it provides sufficient basic anonymous information to guide their initial understanding of the opportunity.

By the same token, we prefer not to provide the Information Memorandum to buyers until both we and our client have satisfied ourselves that there is genuine interest in proceeding to an offer. Normally this will become apparent after the first two meetings;

indeed, often after the first meeting with the prospective buyer. This is because, once we have briefed the client on the outcome of our buyer 'interviews' and determined the final list of parties we agree to proceed with, the client is very knowledgeable about many of the matters that would otherwise have taken some time to understand. Equally, once the vendor has been identified, we will have briefed the buyer so that the first meeting between the vendor and the prospective buyer is a well-focused affair. More often than not, this results in both parties being qualified to arrive at instinctive but informed judgements about the virtue of continuing the process, and an understanding of the path ahead.

Sometimes it takes one further 'getting to know you' chemistry-and-credentials type of session to get to this point, but either way this can then be followed by provision of the Information Memorandum and a process can be agreed for moving forward to an offer.

Some buyers (particularly US buyers) do expect to see the Information Memorandum before the first meeting, and this position therefore has to be taken into consideration. In our experience, however, most buyers accept the way that Results prefers to work; they understand that we would not bring an inappropriate or low-quality business to their attention. If we do come under pressure to produce the memorandum, we are relatively relaxed about doing so, provided that the buyer genuinely believes that this will make the initial meeting more effective from their viewpoint. The potential buyer would also need to be well known to us; we would need to be satisfied as to their professionalism and the seriousness of their intent.

Courtship

As we all know, in any courtship first impressions count for a great deal. The first meeting between vendor and prospective buyer is therefore always the most important one, and it should be prepared for and managed so that by the time it concludes there has been a sufficient meeting of minds (or otherwise) to provide impetus for driving the process forward.

the first meeting is always the most important one

This and subsequent early exploratory meetings should focus not only on dealing with 'chemistry' (critical as this undoubtedly is), but also on the other crucial issues on which both parties need to satisfy themselves, namely:

1 Commercial benefits

Essentially this is about gaining an early understanding of how both parties are going to benefit from a partnership. From the vendor's point of view, the main issue is how their business can achieve incremental growth as a consequence of becoming part of the buyer's organisation. This will increase the vendor's confidence about achieving a successful earn-out.

Key to this understanding is to establish very early in the dialogue why the buyer may be interested in the vendor's business (and the vendor should similarly be ready to reciprocate). This provides early verification of the buyer's intentions, to corroborate what was established during the adviser's earlier 'interview' with them. Any necessary revisions to the positioning of the vendor can also be made.

2 Fit

The Ashridge research made clear that 'fit' is one of the critical success factors (CSFs) in the success of acquisitions. One of the areas most frequently highlighted is parenting style. This means that the acquiring company and its operational units (which may become accountable for the acquired company) need, in many cases, to have much greater self-awareness. In particular, they need to be able to identify characteristics of a vendor's business which will create leverage in making the potential relationship successful.

'fit' is one of the critical success factors in acquisitions

The research produced an excellent process that can be adopted early in the initial exploratory meetings to draw out these characteristics between the parties (see Figure 7 on page 23). With 'fit' as one of the CSFs in acquisition success, the process helps to establish very early on whether there is a sufficient meeting of minds between the prospective parent and 'child'.

The chart in Figure 7 sets out an example of how buyer and vendor can identify and measure the commercial goals and benefits of a potential partnership, thus aligning the partners' ambitions even before the terms of a deal are finalised; indeed, it serves to focus both parties on the deal and its value to them.

Obviously there are other elements of 'fit' to be encompassed in this process, not least strategic fit. In general, the more a deal is done for reasons of financial engineering rather than for reasons of strategic benefit to the existing businesses (the classic '2+2 = 5' concept), the less likelihood there is of success.

If the vendor senses they are simply being acquired for their financial contribution instead of there being any intrinsic value for them in the deal (in terms of increased access to market, skills and methodologies, status, professional development, etc), a natural tendency to focus almost exclusively on the value of the deal will emerge, and money will become an all-consuming preoccupation. If, on the other hand, the buyer and vendor can quickly articulate real strategic and synergistic benefits from the transaction, what often results is a much more rounded and productive debate about the way forward, in which the financial terms, whilst still remaining critical, do not dominate the process. This approach builds trust and confidence between the parties and a much higher probability that deal value and structure will be agreed relatively readily at a level both parties feel is equitable.

the more a deal is done for financial engineering rather than for strategic benefit, the less likelihood there is of success

3 Likely price range and deal structure, payment terms, contractual conditions

While it should not directly be considered as part of the negotiation process, it does make sense for the buyer to be asked early on to express what their approach would be to a deal with the vendor – even if the result is simply an expression of corporate philosophy towards deal-making. It is preferable to get some indication of how acquisition candidates are valued and what price ranges are typically paid for businesses such as the vendor's. This is obviously helpful in gaining an understanding of the parameters of the buyer's interest, and at worst prevents further time being wasted.

4 Personal plans of the vendors

It is clearly critical to the buyer to have an unequivocal understanding of the vendors' personal plans and aspirations affecting their future commitment to the business. The buyer needs to be convinced that the vendor plans to remain with the business during an earn-out, and preferably beyond. If this is not what the vendor has in mind, this needs to be made clear and the buyer given some idea of what plans there are for succession management. It is vital that vendors are completely honest with themselves and with prospective buyers, with whom they must also be seen to be honest.

Any vagueness leads to doubt in the minds of buyers, who will naturally tend to err on the side of caution and assume the worst. If this happens, some buyers will lose all interest immediately. Others, suspecting they are not being told the whole truth, will substantially mark down their valuation because of the perceived risks, particularly if plans for succession are equally vague. It goes without saying, therefore, that this must be one of the best rehearsed issues, about which there can be no ambiguity.

it is vital that vendors are completely honest with themselves and with prospective buyers

5 Personal aspirations, skills and management abilities of the 'mezzanine' layer

Regardless of the answers arising in item 4 above, the buyer will need a clear statement of the plans for succession management and a detailed briefing on the key people involved in the second team management (or 'mezzanine') layer.

One of the most valuable roles that your corporate finance adviser can play during the courtship is to provide a feedback and facilitation process. Being able to make specific observations and ask direct questions of the buyer (questions which might be awkward for future partners to discuss face to face) can be highly productive. It is also important to benefit from the adviser's ability to identify tell-tale signs that may need further probing. This can both move the process on and prevent false expectations. Feedback also enables a clear agenda to be set for each stage of the discussions and limits time-wasting sessions when no one is entirely clear what outcome to expect.

the adviser's ability to identify tell-tale signs can move the process on and prevent false expectations

The other critical role of the adviser is to maintain momentum. This is important, because if the parties do not connect for a number of weeks – distracted by busy daily agendas, holidays or plain sloth – the ground can start to shift in the meantime. If things drag on too long, the various interested parties will get out of step, and the process may need virtually to be started all over again, which is a huge waste of time. Admittedly it is never that easy to keep all the buyer candidates running in parallel at each stage of the process, but not doing so can alienate those who effectively get ahead of the game. These people are left feeling that the vendor is not interested, which may well not be the case. The problem is that buyers have always got something else they can move on to, and if they feel that the vendor's interest is waning it can be very difficult to get back to the top of their priority list.

Getting the offers

Within a couple of months of first approaching the selected candidates, it will usually have become apparent who the serious players are, and final offers will be requested. These should then be analysed on a comparative basis, including a look at the risks involved with each offer. Risks apply in every offer, whether they are to do with the vendor's own ability to achieve the performance levels required, or the terms and method of payment proposed in the offer. These terms will include the form and conditions attached to any securities beyond cash proposed as part of the method of payment, such as loan notes and shares, and conditions attached to proposed earn-out methodologies.

In reviewing both the buyer comparison analysis prepared by the adviser and the proposed negotiating positions, the vendor's initial judgement will be made in part on the rational economic issues, (on which the adviser will have mainly focused), and in part on emotion. These proportions will vary for different individuals, subject to what they are seeking from the sale. The emotional element also has an important rational aspect to it, in that the sense of personal chemistry, cultural, commercial and strategic 'fit', as mentioned earlier, is an extremely important ingredient in deciding whether one parental environment is more conducive to earn-out and career success than another.

In this sense it is important for the vendor to conduct their own due diligence on the candidate organisations at the final furlong of the process, leading up to agreement on the preferred partner. Considerable help with this can be offered by an adviser who has an intimate understanding of the industry and the buyer's businesses. In addition, however, the vendor should request the opportunity to meet previous vendors who have sold to the buyer, and also make discreet enquiries with other contacts already known to the vendor within the buyer organisation.

Getting to the deal

It usually becomes apparent during this review who the final preferred partner will be. The adviser then embarks upon serious and often substantive negotiations with the two or three most serious offers, including the preferred buyer, to get to a final position. In some cases this may take a number of weeks.

Eventually a deal will be agreed in principle and final negotiations can take place over the Heads of Agreement – or Letter of Intent, as the document tends to be called in the USA – setting out all the material points of the agreement. While this is not a legally binding document (other than in clauses regarding confidentiality and exclusivity), it should be regarded as a definitive basis upon which to proceed, and gives the green light to begin employing accountants and lawyers for the due diligence and legal contracts processes.

7

Identifying appropriate buyers

YOUR ADVISER WILL BE ABLE to add considerably to your own knowledge of the prospective buyers, however well you think may know some of them. The adviser's experience may shape a wider understanding of the company from a different perspective; for example, from the corporate/investor (purse strings) perspective, as distinct from the operational end, which may be where your own experience and connections lie. This allows a much richer appreciation of what is really relevant as a 'fit' for your own business.

> **in mature markets most of the main consolidators have already made their acquisitions**

Quite apart from this, if the adviser has real, in-depth knowledge of the sector, then they should have a number of more creative solutions beyond the 'usual suspects'. This is important, since in mature markets such as the UK most of the main consolidators have already made their acquisitions. Accordingly they have limited further acquisition needs in both the main sectors and niche areas, such as healthcare communications. Indeed there is a risk that where they are looking for acquisitions it is to add to their existing 'brands' for remedial or defensive reasons. This obviously necessitates physical mergers, which isn't the most desirable way forward for many owners.

Apart from introducing a wider range of buyer candidates than most vendors could do for themselves, the best advisers will have a close working knowledge of all those companies, including overseas ones (in our industry, this principally means in the USA, Canada, France and Japan, although others are emerging from elsewhere), thereby ensuring that the vendor is well informed about the interests and style of the candidates.

buyers fall into one of two general types: trade and financial

Broadly speaking, buyers fall into one of two general types: trade buyers and financial buyers. There are pros and cons with each.

Trade buyers generally fall into one of four categories:

- Serial buyers, basically the Big Four: WPP, Omnicom, IPG and Publicis.
- Other publicly traded companies, such as Creston, Chime and Incepta in the UK; and a significant number of small to medium-sized North American groups.
- The two major Japanese agency groups, Dentsu and Hakuhodo.
- Other private, unquoted companies, mainly in the USA and UK.

Financial buyers tend to fall into two categories: 'roll-ups' and private equity deals. Actually this is slightly misleading, as roll-ups are often funded by private equity (PE) houses. PE organisations will also buy specific businesses (or at least majority control of them) and support a buy-in team – or else bring in a management team recruited for the purpose – which will either replace or support incumbent management as prospective succession management. This is relatively rare in the UK, but not without precedent.

'Roll-ups' (or 'warehouses' as they are sometimes less attractively known) are a US import. The best known in our sector was Lighthouse (launched by Chicago-based serial roll-up entrepreneur Terry Graunke and sold within a couple of years to the now defunct Cordiant Communications), and its successor, from the same stable of entrepreneurs, DVC (backed by Lake Capital). These vehicles seek to bring a significant number of related businesses together under common ownership, which then benefit from the 'back office' economies and revenue referrals of consolidation.

Clearly these situations are very much geared towards an exit sale to one of the larger consolidators. Five years is usually the kind of timescale envisaged for the return that the funders are seeking, so they are particularly active in the first couple of years, often paying premium prices to ensure they have an established platform on which to 'buy and build'. There is also a tendency, certainly amongst the earlier deals, to limit earn-outs to relatively short periods, sometimes including part-payment in the equity of the vehicle. This

it should always be remembered that the management team itself is a potential buyer

is to ensure they secure partners in the vehicle who will help to build the group, given that they will get a potentially substantial further slice of the cake when the eventual exit is made.

These environments are suited to strongly independent entrepreneurs who share in the vision of what can be achieved financially, and who do not relish the somewhat more established corporate environment of the mainstream consolidators in the market.

It should always be remembered that the management team itself is a potential buyer. This is a legitimate option for many owners, particularly where there is a desire to retire shortly after the deal, and/or where the chances of a trade sale or a strong valuation are slim. The emotional desire to see the business remain 'independent' and owned by loyal, long-serving employees can also be a strong driver for some entrepreneurs. However, for the vendor, careful thought is required before approaching management, as a number of risks attach to this solution, including, but not limited to:

- Management may become distracted from its main task of running the company, thus opening the possibility of a trading decline, and thereby damaging the prospective value of the business.
- There is, in any event, a potential conflict for management in that if trading does fall off, the company could be acquired for a lower price.
- Without competition from other buyers, the price is bound to be less than can be gained from a trade buyer.
- A prospective trade buyer wishing to rely on management to secure a smooth handover could be deterred from competing against management for the deal.

If a buy-out or a trade sale are to be tested at the same time, it is important therefore to secure the potential interest of trade buyers before encouraging management to make its own bid.

8

Deal structures

RELATIVELY FEW APPROACHES ARE USED in acquiring professional service firms such as marketing communications agencies. The most frequently used method is the earn-out.

Earn-out

This provides the buyer with reduced risk, given the vulnerable nature of the intangible assets being acquired, and helps the vendor to achieve optimum value for their business over time. Typically this deal structure comprises an initial payment for the share capital of the target business, based on a fair value on an historic performance basis, augmented by a performance-related valuation paid at the conclusion of the earn-out (sometimes with an interim payment). This payment is usually based on up to five years of subsequent trading, during which time the principals remain firmly in charge of the business, and contracted accordingly. The aim is to reward the vendors for sustaining and growing the profits of the business over time.

The benefits of earn-outs are easily understood, especially in people businesses, subject as they are to the vagaries of human nature. In particular, the buyer knows that the vendors are fully motivated by the prospect of securing full value for their business and so will remain committed over the duration of the earn-out. Yet inherent weaknesses in the concept sub-optimise the viability of many such deals.

Problems with earn-outs

1 Ring-fence syndrome

One major concern is that the much vaunted benefit of synergy – that is, the '2+2 = 5' concept – and all the perceived benefits of integration are largely put on ice during the earn-out. This is because the vendor's lawyers invariably 'ring-fence' the business from the buyer in order that the vendors can maximise the earn-out without risk of interference by the buyer. Even the best of intentions to provide introductions to other group companies and clients may be resisted by the buyer, anxious that if anything goes wrong they will risk the goodwill of such group companies or even lose clients.

the earn-out often has the opposite effect to the one intended

This can also be used as a (not unreasonable) excuse by the buyer. The concern may be that by introducing business into the acquired company – particularly if it cannibalises existing business – they are at risk of paying a multiple on profits that they could probably have made within their existing organisation.

The earn-out, therefore, very often has the opposite effect to the one an acquisition is intended to have, and can limit both parties' potential for leveraging the relationship.

2 Deferral or incentive?

Although an earn-out corresponds to the subsequent performance of the target company, the payment is made to the original vendors in line with individual shareholding interests at the time of sale. Earn-outs are not generally designed to reward non-shareholders at the time of sale, largely for tax-related reasons. Taxation obligations regarding earn-outs are usually satisfied by the buyer issuing loan notes (see Chapter 13) or its own shares. However, the latter is more often to mitigate the buyer's risk and particularly to secure commitment by the vendor. The buyer will also want to see in place appropriate incentives for key employees, whether through the earn-out or otherwise.

3 Post earn-out syndrome

For vendors working through an earn-out, there is an understandable temptation to view all expenditure in terms of its multiplier effect. Accordingly the focus may well be on achieving relatively short-term profits at the expense of longer-term investment in the business. This applies particularly in the years preceding interim and final earn-out payments. The result is there is a real risk of a slump in business in the year following completion of the earn-out – exaggerated still further by the vendors' departure, if this happens. The damage to relationships

there is a real risk of a slump in the year following completion of the earn-out

with clients and staff caused by this lack of investment is one of the most common complaints with earn-outs. Fortunately it is not all that difficult for buyers to address.

One approach is to average out the earnings across the duration of the earn-out. But although this can limit the worst of the downside of this syndrome, a more effective strategy exists. Research from Ashridge found greater dividends are achieved by re-thinking the performance measures used by buyers during the earn-out. Traditionally financial, these measures are by definition lagging indicators of performance. With a relationship-based business, however, the real measures required must be leading indicators. On the basis, therefore, of 'what you measure is what you get', the emphasis should instead be on measurement of employee engagement and client satisfaction, as there is a substantive body of evidence demonstrating a clear link between high levels of both these dimensions and strong, sustainable financial performance.[1]

It is perfectly possible to obtain relatively inexpensive, independently audited provision of such measures on a regular basis. And because they provide clear predictive indications of performance at both individual client and staffing level, the measures enable a proactive rather than reactive correcting strategy. In fact they constitute sound operational policy, earn-out or not.

Such actions are even more effective when used in the same way as financial measures as a means of determining the earn-out payment. For example, there is no reason why achievement of specific levels of client satisfaction cannot result in variation of the multiple used

---

1 James L. Heskett et al., 'Putting the service–profit chain to work', *Harvard Business Review*, March–April 1994.

for exit payments being based on industry or group level bench-marks, with a bonus for an upper quartile ranking.

This approach effectively aligns the goals of both buyer and vendor. On the one hand, the vendor recognises the importance of strong investment in client and employee engagement in improving the financial return. On the other, the buyer can be more confident of robust business health at completion of the earn-out. The likelihood of sustainability is far higher than is typically the case, regardless of how well buyers motivate vendors in the post earn-out environment.

4 Share 'overhang'

If the consideration for earn-out payments is to be made in the acquiring company's shares, or if the buyer cannot afford to pay in cash and makes shares the primary option, this can cause great difficulties if the buyer's financial circumstances or market conditions are unfavourable at the time of the pay-out. If the share price is much reduced, and/or the vendor company has been particularly successful in growing profits substantially during the earn-out (possibly while the rest of the group has floundered), the number of shares issued may be so large as to make the vendor a major shareholder in the company. Not only may this be highly undesirable from the vendor's perspective, it is equally undesirable for the investor shareholders in the buyer. This is because the likely effect of this share 'overhang' will be to hold down the buyer's share price in the markets, creating a self-fulfilling decline in its business as it is held back from further investment while this scenario endures.

In order to avoid this trap, a number of relatively simple devices can be used. Most commonly a 'cap' is placed on the maximum amount to be paid and the balance of shares and cash paid under the earn-out is at the option of the buyer, in order to limit the buyer's exposure. In addition, the final consideration is usually based on an average performance over time rather than on one specific year, which may have benefited from some form of 'super-profit' situation.

A less used but also effective tool is to vary the multiple to be paid for earn-outs in relation to the multiple applying to the buyer's stock at the time of the payout. An example would be to agree no variation as long as the buyer's multiple remains above, say, 16, but below this the vendor is asked to agree to a 1-point drop in their exit multiple for each 2-point drop in the parent company's multiple. Clearly this is a controversial proposition, but arguably entirely sensible from the buyer's perspective.

Accordingly it is possible to minimise the risks that undermine the earn-out's perceived benefits of aligned commitment. Perhaps unsurprisingly, however, in the light of these difficulties alternative methodologies continue to be used, two of which are part-acquisition and outright acquisition.

Part-acquisition

While I have sought to focus this book on 100 per cent transactions, which form the majority of transactions in the marcoms industry, there is no doubt that there is also a role for part-acquisitions, which are structured as part of a longer term agreement for an eventual complete sale.

Typically this involves the buyer acquiring less than 100 per cent of the company, though usually a majority (in the UK, 75 per cent is the preferred minimum, given that below this it is not possible to consolidate a group's trading for maximum tax efficiency). Under normal circumstances the value is paid 'up-front' for the shares acquired and there is no earn-out as such. The acquirer then gains the option to 'call', and grants the right for the shareholders to 'put' the balance of the shares after a period of years or when triggered by some other event such as achievement of specified financial performance.

Despite what has previously been said about taxation, on occasion significant minority stakes are taken by buyers. These are usually linked to options as indicated above, where the move is to gain a presence in, and experience of, a new market sector. Over the years, Omnicom has proceeded in this way in a number of sectors, such as PR, technology marketing and new media. More recently, the second largest Japanese group,

on occasion significant minority stakes are taken by buyers

Hakuhodo, has pursued this policy in developing its international acquisitions, with purchases in the UK (Mustoe Merriman), Germany, the USA, and shortly in Spain. In some cases this may also be a way of securing the acquisition of an important strategic partner (such as for client reasons) that is unwilling to give up control at the time that the buyer wishes to proceed. It should be noted that the value per share for a minority position will generally be less than when control is obtained.

Where such transactions are initiated, they will generally avoid many of the issues of an earn-out, but they do present their own challenges. For example, once a substantial shareholding has been sold it is very difficult, though not impossible, to contemplate the value of the balance of the shares ultimately being sold to the buyer. Therefore it is very important at the outset to agree what the exit strategy is – in respect of timing and valuation – otherwise the vendor will have very limited bargaining power when finally seeking to realise value for the balance. Equally, full agreement must be reached, usually via a shareholders' agreement, on management control covering such matters as senior management appointments and compensation, capital expenditure, profit distributions, office relocation, handling competitive clients, and so on.

It is sometimes felt appropriate to leave a proportion of the shares, say 20 per cent, in the hands of the vendors upon a sale. This serves as effectively the equivalent of securing an earn-out payment after an agreed period of time, or as part of the earn-out structure. This is not an unreasonable proposition. Sometimes public companies shy away from having minority stakes held by subsidiary companies, seeing this as 'untidy' in terms of both ownership and unquantifiable contingent liabilities. Vendors sometimes feel uncomfortable with the notion of a minority stake in 'their' company and see little point in it. But this tends to occur most when the buyer hasn't really thought through the purpose and exit strategy of such an approach. All the same, these minus points seem to be relatively insignificant and can often be overcome through negotiation if the deal is important enough to both parties.

However, it should be noted that for US buyers, under new Sarbanes-Oxley rules, the concept of options has been effectively eliminated due to the effect of changes to goodwill accounting, and in the UK has been thrown into disarray due to recent capital gains tax (CGT) changes, meaning that there is now a real risk that payments can be deemed to be employment rather than capital related. This clearly results in a dramatic impact on tax payments given the UK's virtually universal 10% capital gains tax regime. Clearly the role of the tax adviser is being elevated by these unfortunate developments.

Outright acquisition

In a few cases, buyers have made a full commitment to making major strategic acquisitions outright without a conventional earn-out, in order to secure full operating control and integration from day one.

However, even here the vendors have continued to be motivated either by receipt of a significant percentage of the acquisition price in shares, and/or by receiving further 'bonus' shares for reaching pre-agreed performance targets. In these situations the vendors have tended to buy into a very clear exit strategy for the whole 'group' from the outset. One of the best examples in the UK was the Lighthouse venture, which was eventually sold to Cordiant.

the onus is on the buyer to de-risk the transaction by extensive due diligence beyond the conventional areas

Chime Communications was an interesting example of a short earn-out philosophy, with mixed success, while in the market research sector, Taylor Nelson Sofres (TNS to its friends), the large publicly quoted international research group, has averaged about five transactions a year across the world, and increasingly avoids earn-outs, or pursues very short earn-out periods.

In these situations the onus is on the buyer to de-risk the transaction by extensive due diligence beyond the conventional legal and financial areas, or to acquire particularly large companies with their own established market momentum and little dependence on specific individuals or clients, or the economic cycle.

9

Getting to the valuation

THERE IS NO EXACT SCIENCE when it comes to valuing a private, unquoted people business, where the majority of what is paid is for intangible assets, principally goodwill. Goodwill is essentially the sustainable momentum of trading profits based on reputation and standing in the marketplace and the durability of relationships with clients, employees, suppliers and partnerships. Inevitably there is significant

risk assessment is the most demanding aspect of valuation

scope for disagreement as to value, even between willing buyer and vendor, where judgement about these assets is largely in the eye of the beholder. Given the vulnerability of assets that are primarily dependent upon the motivation of owners, managers and staff over time, it is not surprising that risk assessment is the most demanding aspect of valuation, and it is in this area in particular that some sophistication can be applied.

Although there is always an element of subjectivity in valuation, some advisers operate only in one sector and bring a wealth of informed knowledge and experience of the market to bear in assessing the range of potential discount and premium factors which can apply. It is wrong to believe that there is any right answer until it is proven in the marketplace with competitive bids on the table. Indeed, without competitive bids it is impossible to tell whether a bid from a single prospective buyer is the right or best answer.

it is wrong to believe that there is any right answer until it is proven in the marketplace

It is also important to understand that every business, indeed every deal, has its own unique circumstances, and it is therefore difficult to reach conclusions about value merely via comparison with other apparently similar transactions (although of course this can be one ingredient in the overall judgement of value). Equally, press and (particularly) hearsay versions of deal values are almost always grossly misleading, due to either inappropriate or selective use of information, or inadequate knowledge and understanding of the facts.

Real value lies in the future. The past belongs to the owners, and only serves as a clue to current value and the risks associated with a projection of what really matters to a buyer: future profits and cash flows.

Share ownership

Different classes of shares can have different values, depending upon the rights and obligations attached to them, such as voting, dividend and capital gains rights. It is therefore very important to ensure the most appropriate share structure exists to meet the needs both of the owners (which may well need to be different for founders and subsequent shareholders) and of the business (such as legislating for outside development capital and incentives for succession management).

Methods of valuation

There are at least four methods of valuation of businesses, two of which are very common in the marcoms industry:

1 P/E multiples

For low asset, people-based businesses, the most common form of valuation is capitalised earnings, involving the application of a price earnings (P/E) multiple to the maintainable earnings in the business. Traditionally this was based on profits after tax (and before dividends), but, increasingly, pre-tax profits tend to be used as the basis. Even earnings before interest and tax (EBIT) can be used. Whichever arithmetical basis is used, the outcome is effectively the same.

'adjusted' profits are the normal base upon which any multiple is applied

The two issues which buyer and vendor will generally debate most are the base profitability to which the multiple is applied, and the multiple itself.

Normally there are a number of adjustments to be made in order to 'normalise' the financials in readiness for a going forward position under new ownership. For example, exceptional costs (such as for redundancies or removal of a director), interest, and proprietor's excess remuneration, bonuses and expenses (beyond the cost of employing an executive in the open market to perform there duties), will all be removed in order to arrive at a sustainable cost base and 'clean' trading result. 'Adjusted' profits are therefore the normal base upon which any multiple is applied.

As to the multiple itself, a good starting point is the media section of the *Financial Times* UK stock market prices to see the multiples being applied to the quoted stocks in the sector (such as WPP in the UK). These typically average around 20 on historic performance (i.e. the last year's published results) over the long term. Unfortunately they have little relevance to small, privately held companies with no liquidity in their shares, who do not have the demanding treadmill of growth per share required by institutional shareholders. The accepted starting point therefore for valuing a high performing, substantial growth private company would be about half of the public company equivalent. Companies without a similar critical mass and growth perspective, that are often reliant upon a relatively small number of key clients and business 'drivers', are even more vulnerable and higher risk, and are therefore unlikely to command multiples at this end of the spectrum – indeed they may be discounted by up to a further 50 per cent, i.e. a quarter of the publicly quoted stocks.

There is also much misleading talk about multiples paid for acquisition of private companies. Hearsay of multiples of 10–12, for example, may well be true for exceptional businesses, but even then it is likely to refer to after-tax profits, where the equivalent pre-tax multiple would probably be nearer to 7–9.

Indeed, this would tend to be the top end for the very best companies in the sector under normal circumstances, with more typical multiples seen at around 4–6 times adjusted pre-tax profits (6–8 times post-tax profits). Of course, this is inflated for periods at the top of a bull market, but these are usually fairly short-lived. The norm for a mid-sized, consistently well performing modest growth company would therefore be in the region of a 5 × multiple on pre-tax profits (7 on post-tax).

A high initial multiple can be rapidly undermined by the failure of promised growth rates in the face of a bear market (which always follows a heady bull market), and the consequent non-delivery of earn-outs. The related loss of motivation of the vendors usually leads to the complete failure of the whole relationship, and in these circumstances nearly everyone is a loser.

a high initial multiple can be undermined by the failure of promised growth

2 Revenue multiples

Alternatively, in some essentially fee-based businesses, such as PR or design, valuation can be based on a percentage of the gross fees or income (usually referred to as revenue by US buyers), and this can also prove appropriate in merger situations. However, the arithmetic effectively works back to similar numbers whichever method is used. Thus for high performing, usually large, businesses, a factor of perhaps 125 per cent multiplied by revenue could be applied, or, to put it another way, a multiple of revenue of 1.25.

To work through an example, take a business earning 15 per cent operating margin on gross profit (revenue) of £1m, i.e. £150,000 profit before tax (PBT). At a tax rate of 35 per cent (roughly the effective tax rate of most buyers), a multiple of 10 × the post-tax £100,000 is equivalent to 1 × revenue. The PBT multiple (to save you doing the sums) is 6.7 – a highly unlikely value incidentally for such a small company.

3 Return on investment (ROI)

A sanity check for a buyer, and a means for the vendor to gain realistic expectations of value, is to examine ROI. Most companies will have a view on an acceptable return on capital invested in the business, and an acquisition should be no different. Typically this is likely to be in the 15–20 per cent per annum range. ROI would tend to be defined as the adjusted earnings (profits) before interest and tax (EBIT) as a percentage of the capital employed. The capital is the sum of the acquisition cost and the cost of the funds, less the cash flow generated by the acquired business.

The required rate of return can be applied to the projected EBIT to calculate the maximum acquisition price that can be afforded, dependent upon various optional scenarios.

In simple terms, a vendor can work out for themselves what a buyer ought to be able to afford to pay, ignoring any calculation for risk and premium pricing benefits from economic synergies. For every £1m of cash the buyer might agree to pay, it is likely that the cost of this money is something up to £100,000 each year (even in today's low interest climate), however it is funded. This is less, of course, the receipt of the net cash generation, after tax, from the acquired business.

for every £1m of cash the buyer might agree to pay, the cost is up to £100,000 p.a.

4 Discounted cash flow (DCF)

Cash is king in all businesses, and particularly where debt is a significant basis for funding acquisitions. A DCF calculation of value would therefore in theory appear to be useful in our industry, where debt is frequently employed. That said, we see little obvious evidence of this, although one would imagine that the bean counters responsible for analysing acquisitions and preparing offers would resort to such methodologies as a sanity check.

As above, the purchase consideration is taken as equivalent to capital expenditure. This approach values a business by the present value of future cash flows from the company. A discount rate is applied as a measure of the risk in achieving the projected cash flows.

The net cash flow for each year is aggregated from the operating profits of the acquired business, the working capital and capex employed. Software programs are then used in conjunction with various options prepared from sensitivity analysis to assess the cash flow generated across the period of the earn-out. This will reveal the extent to which an adequate return is achieved to satisfy the banks, where borrowing is involved, and the company's own shareholder needs.

Which to choose?

Whichever approach is used (and typically at least two will be), the value of a business cannot be reduced to a simple formula, as a complex series of issues about the business must be analysed objectively, relying on market experience and drawing upon a detailed database of previous transactions for comparison purposes. The different approaches above will often produce somewhat different valuations for a specific company. This is entirely acceptable, and is why valuations should be expressed as a range, rather than a specific figure, which will simply lack credibility.

From the buyer's viewpoint it also explains how they will have arrived at an opening bid offer, and suggests just how far they can go in negotiation before over-paying.

Regardless of the methods used, to achieve the strongest value the vendor must have many strong premium values and virtually no discount factors. The main factors vendors should aim to address in their businesses prior to their intended sale are listed below. These values are achieved over many years and vendors will gain the maximum value by adopting a long-term strategy that embraces them.

the vendor must have strong premium values and virtually no discount factors

Premium values

Scarcity

There are particular qualities which will often have special value for certain buyers because they are in scarce supply, at least from an acquisition viewpoint. Indeed a buyer who fails to complete a transaction with such companies – particularly where it is acquired by a major competitor – faces a number of possible threats. These include:

1 Reputation. 'One can live down anything except a good reputation,' said Oscar Wilde. Maybe, but in our industry reputation is based on brand values that are hard won over time.

Service brands are predominantly about people, experience, knowledge and relationships. Clearly a robust culture usually underpins a strong reputation, which in turn provides a potent competitive position. The values that bind these qualities together helps create a reputation in the marketplace, and the confidence such a business exudes is all-pervading and magnetic in its appeal to clients and staff alike.

This often manifests itself in proprietary skill sets and methodologies and the resultant value charging and accompanying margins. These intangibles usually also provide real scope for scaleability – a difficulty in many agencies, where growth is limited by a lack of assets capable of leverage beyond the abilities of the founders.

Most businesses with a strong reputation tend to have a very distinctive proposition in the marketplace, whether this is in a specialised niche or as a generalist. The proposition may be a strategically driven positioning, a strong results orientation, or use of proprietary skills or tools that are not easily replicated by competitors. Alternatively, it may just be a very strong, very well merchandised culture. This can simply be the product of the personalities of the founders, however, and this may lead buyers to the opposite view about value, should they conclude the business is too heavily dependent upon such people (see 'Discount factors' on pages 89 to 96).

2 Blue-chip clients. There will be some clients in a buyer's portfolio – or some clients whom they wish to attract – for whom the buyer needs to provide a greater range or depth of service, sometimes in a new location. That said, interest will be limited if the relationship is in a narrow or superficial category, is project driven, or is otherwise not very well secured. Indeed,

in such situations the buyer may well ask themselves, why make a purchase to secure trade from a client with whom they may already have a superior relationship and when they could conceivably win the client's business without having to buy it?

3 Proprietary properties. If the company has developed specific rights, tools, software, methodologies or other intellectual property that is not readily available in the market and/or is ahead of the competition, including the buyer, there is a real premium value to a buyer. The benefit of saving even a year of development time could be considerable to the buyer.

4 Long–term client contracts. One risk associated with much of the industry is relatively short client tenure and the contractual position this implies. There are, though, exceptional contract situations, often in outsourced scenarios, as experienced in some database, fulfilment and call centre businesses, for example. In these instances the buyer obviously has greater confidence about the substance of future income projections.

5 Niche positioning. Clearly a niche can be so small that there is no market in it; in general however, specialist businesses, particularly those in long-term growth industries such as healthcare, are able to command a strong reputation, premium pricing and long-term client relationships – quite apart from the all-important growth perspective. In comparison, general market businesses find it very difficult to create a sustainable proposition; one that provides buyers with the same level of confidence that would justify a higher price than a specialist equivalent business.

It is clear, therefore, that a vendor who can create such scarce assets and identify buyers for whom these will satisfy real 'need' drivers (as opposed to 'nice to have' criteria) will have real pricing power with such buyers.

Goodwill

Goodwill is at the core of value in people businesses, as previously explained, and essentially represents the quality of relationships between the company and its various audiences. Goodwill's two key features are employee engagement (as manifested in modest staff turnover, advocacy, training, etc) and client retention. As detailed in Chapter 3, these are known drivers of growth and are more and more likely to become recognised as such by buyers in this industry. Vendors who can demonstrate high, increasing levels of client satisfaction through independent measures are likely to command premium values.

> goodwill's two key features are employee engagement and client retention

The ideal is evidence of a strong track record over several years, such that the business can be seen to be assuming a life of its own, independent of the founders. This is often referred to as becoming institutionalised. An unfortunate expression, perhaps, but a state of self-perpetuation helps give the buyer real confidence that earnings should be at least broadly maintainable.

Another way of interpreting these matters is by looking at the strength and depth of management that the buyer is being invited to back. Also important in this context is the spread of client relationships – that is, individual clients who are not dependent on one key person.

Synergy

Synergy is a word subject to mistrust and the meaning of which is much abused. Yet where synergy genuinely exists it is a powerful driver of growth and value. It can be achieved through cost savings, stronger management or increased revenue from a shared client, as is often the case in a merger. In this event, the vendor is right to argue that the increased value created by the transaction should be at least shared with the vendor, without which the benefits could not be achieved.

Careful analysis of the synergies that can be realised can set one offer apart from others on the table. It pays the buyer to investigate these benefits, which can then justify a potential value over and above competitor bids.

That said, a buyer should be cautious about glib statements of cross-referral synergies. They rarely happen, and indeed the earn-out scenario works counter to this, as described in Chapter 8. There is a very real danger in making assumptions about the impact on the opportunities to maximise earn-outs based on such sweeping statements. Indeed, this is a classic example of how a buyer is not managing expectations correctly, incurring all the attendant risks of subsequent loss of goodwill and motivation.

where synergy genuinely exists it is a powerful driver of growth and value

Timing

Good timing can be a source of premium value. One example would be where the buyer gains a short-cut to market from acquiring intellectual capital, or other assets or skills which facilitate a perceived need to change or acquire a competitive advantage. Similarly, a pressing client-driven need at a particular moment can prove a powerful driver of value.

Timing also relates to the point in the company's growth cycle when a sale is contemplated. As shown in Figure 9, on page 36, it is clear that selling when the business is barely out of nappies is unlikely to create much value. The business is relatively unproven, with no real track record or reputation, and will be considered as high risk by the buyer, which will in turn be reflected in a low valuation.

Equally, selling at the top of the imaginary growth cycle, which buyers normally assume applies to any business, can be just as poor a judgement to make. There is often an assumption that selling when profits have gone about as far as they can go will maximise the return. Unfortunately this rarely works, as the buyer soon realises that the business is at risk of going ex-growth, which can severely limit their view on the multiple, driven largely by perceptions of growth rate during the earn-out. This in turn determines the ROI required, which usually varies between 15 and 20 per cent per annum (about half that of a venture capitalist, incidentally). Low growth expectation obviously pushes the timescale, and therefore the investment return on the transaction, far out into the future. Bearing this in mind, the scope for a high valuation is clearly limited. Yet that is exactly what such vendors assume they will receive after having established a profitable business, maybe over many years.

> there is often an assumption that selling when profits have gone about as far as they can will maximise the return

The chance of substantial disappointment in these situations is therefore high, and sure enough this scenario has led to a number of disasters in our industry. Usually vendors have held out for a price they were never going to get, until the business atrophies and/or is hit by economic downturn, rarely recovering afterwards.

Predictably then, the optimum valuation point exists somewhere between these two extremes. Even though the absolute amount of profitability is lower than at the peak, the multiple to be applied will be greater because of the buyer's anticipation of strong growth. By taking into account both the probable earlier completion of the earn-out (usually two or three years) and a quality-of-life dimension, it can be calculated that a greater return is likely to be achieved.

Finally, as observed earlier, when making a judgement about timing it is important to be aware of the effects of the economic cycle, which are always difficult to call and can easily muddy the waters.

Scale

It is oversimplifying matters to say that larger businesses automatically achieve higher multiples, but there is a strong general shift in this direction. The primary reason is one of simple economics. At one end of the argument, the cost to a buyer of managing and financing an acquisition is generally much the same regardless of the scale. At the other is the fact that the larger and more 'institutionalised' the acquired business is, the more the risks tend to diminish.

Consequently, as profits expand consistently beyond £500,000, and particularly beyond £1m pbt, this more economic model can be expected to lead to higher multiples.

Growth

Growth, preferably of the double-digit variety, ultimately drives premium valuations, which will generally be evidenced or facilitated by the previous points. As indicated elsewhere, though, we are talking of future growth, for which historic earnings are merely one aspect of the evidence. Indeed, as also mentioned earlier, the prospect of a business going ex-growth is always something that will see value marked down heavily. In particular, a business that has been creating exceptional profit margins in the two or three years prior to sale can create the suspicion that it has been 'pumped up' for sale, with unsustainable over-charging and limited investment.

The real issue in achieving a high valuation will be evidence of continuing strong growth, as derived from a good market reputation, a competitive offer, specific intellectual properties, and driven, ambitious, highly motivated and talented managers.

Strong, consistent, preferably recession-resistant, growth in earnings justifies a full price, because the acquirer can be assured of good visibility in determining a return on their investment.

Summary

Fulfilling these premium values is simply the consequence of satisfying buyers that the risk to their investment is minimal. Therefore, the more vendors can plan to deliver buyers with such properties, the more they can expect to realise full value.

Discount factors

By contrast, where these virtues do not exist, vendors may need to adjust their value expectations accordingly. Indeed, not being in a position to offer a business with some combination of scarcity, scale, strong reputation and client retention will see substantial discount value, by as much as 50 per cent. Other factors which will create further discounting can be briefly identified as follows.

High gearing

Most businesses in the sector can be run on a cash generative basis, so heavy borrowings will tend to indicate an unprofitable or poorly managed business. In addition, buyers are not normally attracted to increasing their own gearing, which may affect their ability to invest in their own business and fund further acquisitions. If a buyer is prepared to proceed, such debt will almost certainly be deducted from the purchase price.

Poor financial management

Lack of adequate financial controls and information will severely reduce the buyer's confidence in what they are being told, and increase the perception of risk in the business. It is especially important (as mentioned previously) that the buyer sees that there is a financial director in the business who they feel is reliable and with whom they believe they can work well.

Contingent liabilities

Long-term liabilities, exemplified usually by property leases, are a very real depressant to value. The buyer will be suspicious that if something went wrong with the business, they could, for example, be left with a 10-year lease at £250,000 a year, or whatever, creating a serious drain on earnings. Sadly, numerous examples of this continue to litter our industry. Even without a doomsday scenario, the inflexibility imposed by a long, unbreakable lease will impact negatively on a new owner, who will have to accommodate changes brought about by expansion, contraction, mergers, and so on. Needless to say it will therefore result in a discounted view of value.

lack of adequate financial controls and information will severely reduce the buyer's confidence

Other liabilities may not have the same level of risk attached; nonetheless, legal due diligence teams will also be searching for liabilities in respect of pensions, outstanding litigation, supplier contracts, and other similar contingencies.

Contractual fraud

This is another trap into which the unwary can fall, and is particularly onerous. There has been a push for greater accountability in business over the last decade, increased intervention by client procurement managers, and a more generally litigious environment. Together with the emergence of client contracts that specify unequivocally what fees and charges can and cannot be made, these developments brought about a new era of transparency to the industry. Agencies hid for many years behind a widespread

91

commission system. Although this has largely disappeared, its legacy unfortunately still endures in some long-established businesses. These seek to secure 'super-profit' by effectively charging for aspects of their service that are expressly forbidden in their client contracts. Receiving commissions from suppliers, such as printers and production houses for example, would be highly questionable in such circumstances.

Most buyers, particularly quoted companies, will simply not countenance such practices, and would probably walk away from a deal where there is evidence of such behaviour. At the very least, they would expect to reduce the profits of the company for the purpose of valuation, on the basis that such activities cease upon completion of the transaction. They would also expect the vendors to undertake to meet any claims which subsequently arise. However, such warranties are only half the issue for a buyer, who worries that the reputation of the business could be damaged, clients lost, and management time distracted by dealing with claims. Consequently value will be both severely discounted and heavily predicated on future performance.

At Results, we have seen all this come as a great shock to some vendors, who suddenly find a substantially profitable business decimated in value because of their unwise behaviour over the years in exploiting their clients. Such activity is moreover clearly fraudulent, and the risks of criminal prosecution are relatively high in the current climate of crackdowns against corporate excesses.

Unsustainable margins

Where the operating margins in the business are in excess of, say,

25 per cent of the gross margin (or revenue), the buyer's suspicions will be aroused, unless it is evident the margins have been sustained over a long period of time. The buyer is only interested in what is likely to be the continuing position, and will closely examine high margins over, say, a two or three year period, as these may have been gained at the expense of the client work, or the proper level of investment in people, creativity, and the product in general.

a buyer will quickly realise whether he is dealing with a well-advised and knowledgeable vendor

Naive vendors

A buyer will quickly realise whether he is dealing with a reasonable, well-advised and knowledgeable vendor. If it becomes apparent early on in the proceedings that the vendor has unreasonable value expectations and/or has limited understanding of the acquisition process, the buyer will rapidly lose interest. Buyers simply do not have the time or the inclination to educate a vendor and/or his advisers on the realities of value and process. At best, they may simply make a 'low-ball' offer in the anticipation that nothing more will come of it – if for no other reason than being seen to have gone through the motions.

For this reason there is a general preference for vendors to be well advised by a respected intermediary, because this both economises on the whole process, and also brings into the equation someone who will manage the vendor's expectations sensibly, while rigorously pursuing their best overall interests.

One or two buyers, however, take rather a short-sighted attitude to advisers, believing that their intervention creates an auction that forces them to pay higher prices than necessary. At Results, our response to this is to take it as a compliment. But we would also express concern that such firms do not appear to have sufficient confidence in the rigour of their own processes to forestall any chance of overpaying. This moreover implies that such firms are aiming to underpay if they can get away with it. In our view, this is a strategy that will and can often return to haunt the buyer, it being human nature for people who feel they have been taken advantage of to subsequently seek to get their own back. The earn-out system is especially vulnerable to exploitation by those so inclined.

incentive schemes established close to acquisition can now be treated more unfavourably under taxation law

Lack of succession management

This is a serious flaw in the eyes of a buyer, who needs to be confident that there is the prospect of well-motivated managers to take over successfully from the current drivers of the business. But the identification and development of such individuals is only one aspect of this. Of equal importance is the manner in which they are incentivised, and this needs to have been planned and thought through a long time before the sale. Incentive schemes established close to the acquisition date can now be treated much more unfavourably under taxation law. Understandably in this case, the buyer will expect to deduct any additional costs incurred from the consideration being paid to the vendors of the business.

Age of the vendors

This factor is obvious to most people – although strangely not always to people in their 50s. Like it or not, these vendors are perceived as having retirement in their sights, which in turn suggests their ambition has been blunted. Vendors in their 40s are therefore generally more attractive to acquirers; with this in mind, their older counterparts must be seen to have in place an established succession plan with key people in senior positions of responsibility, who are well motivated to perform over the long term. Without evidence of these measures the business could be subject to serious discount.

Heavy reliance on one client

If the revenue of one client equates to more than the operating margin of the business, so that its loss can wipe out profits at a stroke, buyers will heavily discount value and quite often walk away from a deal altogether.

Weak positioning or strategy

Given the need for strong growth post-acquisition, businesses that have little point of difference to offer the market and no clear and discernible strategy to secure competitive advantage have limited appeal to most buyers. The exception may be in a merger scenario, where the business is acquired largely for economic purposes. These situations are comparatively rare, but can present such vendors with the best prospects for negotiating a reasonable valuation.

Unclear, unfocused assets

Often a by-product of the previous problem, unclear assets occur when entrepreneurs feel it necessary to build a range of services around their core business either as a means of securing greater share of budget from the client, or to grow the business generally, or as a defensive move. Whatever the rationale, this strategy is often ill-advised – not least because there are relatively few examples of it proving to be successful operationally. In fact it can actually threaten the core business, as key fee-earning managers become distracted. The risk is that businesses are started with limited knowledge outside the established area of expertise, and are under-capitalised, and fail or perform in a mediocre manner, which further drains the parent business of resource.

Even where this strategy is reasonably successful, however, at sale it can have the opposite outcome to the one intended. A many-headed hydra muddies the water for the typical buyer, who may be examining a number of investments at any particular time, probably with much clearer strategic goals, usually in specific discipline areas. If the buyer cannot very quickly see that the business is a 'pure-play' example of what he is shopping for, the file will go in the 'too difficult' tray. And, almost regardless of performance, there it is likely to stay unless a heavily discounted price is deemed acceptable.

To be fair, this becomes less of a problem with scale – where operating profits are well in excess of £2m, say – because there are probably opportunities to demerge units of the business into separate alignments within the buyer's existing portfolio of businesses. But, even so, anything that presents such complications tends to suffer, at least to some degree, in valuation terms.

Profit & loss

It is important to focus on two areas of the P&L in particular, when preparing the accounts for valuation.

Adjusted operating earnings

This involves past performance, and its projection forward. Current earnings are the profits earned after subtracting operating costs (e.g. payroll, rent, benefits, office, expenses) from commission and fee revenues. Operating earnings are often expressed as EBIT (as mentioned earlier).

Operating expenses generally do not include interest income or expenses, taxes and the purchase of large one-off capital equipment (e.g. computers). Operating earnings are usually adjusted to remove owner benefits that would normally not be available if the agency were a wholly owned subsidiary of a larger company. Owner benefits could include such items as company-owned boats or holiday homes, and personal expenses.

The earnings can also be adjusted to remove major non-recurring, non-trading expenses such as redundancy, loss of office payments, litigation and expenses of moving office, as well as the costs of advisers involved specifically in the sale of the business. While the last is not usually in question, it is fair to say there can often be quite difficult debate about the acceptability of others of these 'add-backs'.

Profit margin

The relative quality of these earnings is measured by the profit margin. For well-run agencies, this margin can range from 15 per cent of revenues to as high as 30 per cent of revenues.

An agency with a consistent growth rate in excess of 10 per cent over a period of three or more years can argue in favour of applying the multiple to the average earnings for the current and the previous year, or even just the current year. Exceptionally, some agencies and marketing services businesses growing very rapidly (20 per cent or more per annum) have been able to support an earnings dimension based solely on earnings forecasted for the current year. Selection of the representative operating profit is a key step in an appraisal, and even though it involves quantitative data, the reader should understand that its selection is based on qualitative judgement.

Balance sheet

So far nothing has been said about the balance sheet. This is primarily because it is rarely valued for itself in acquisitions of people businesses. Clearly if there are shareholder funds in excess of the working capital needs of the business, these will be acquired at face value, i.e. on a pound-for-pound basis as the most tax-efficient means of extracting such shareholder funds. The great advantage of leaving such funds in the business until the sale is that they are effectively extracted as part of the sale consideration. This means they are (subject to the present favourable taper relief) liable to only 10 per cent capital gains rather than the 40 per cent charged on dividends and bonuses.

debt in people businesses is generally regarded as a sign of poor financial management

As indicated under 'Discount factors' above, debt in people businesses is generally regarded as a sign of poor financial management, although of course there are perfectly legitimate occasions for taking on debt – such as buying out shareholders, or business-transforming capital investments (including acquisitions). Beyond this, however, any debt that is to be assumed by the buyer will be directly deducted from the payments the buyer makes to the shareholders. In the same way, any short-term bank borrowings that are in more or less continuous use will be counted as long-term debt in the same way.

Cash or shares

One final factor affecting value really only comes to bear in the nego-tiation: this is the extent to which the consideration is paid through the transfer of shares in the buyer's company rather than cash (or cash equivalent securities). Shares obviously carry an element of risk in a way that cash does not, in that share prices go up and down over time and may be denominated in another currency. Consequently, a buyer offering shares will need to increase value somewhat to counteract this risk. Clearly it is for the vendors to satisfy themselves as to the wisdom of a shares 'gamble', noting as they will that usually the shares cannot be 'cashed' until at least 12 months from issue or even until the end of the earn-out. In making such a judgement, the vendors must take into account the quality of the buyer's stock rating over time; the relative liquidity of the shares, particularly on a 'junior' market such as AIM or OFEX in the UK; and the timing of the economic cycle. None of these are neces-sarily easy to judge, and nor can any comfort in respect of them be expected from the buyer.

Accordingly, the tendency is to insist on as much cash as possible. The effect of the 2000 market crash on most of the industry's stock prices makes this view even less surprising – but frankly that says something about the logic of selling at the top of the cycle, which I have already remarked on elsewhere in this book. Unfortunately, in many instances, the result of a cash-only requirement by a vendor is to dramatically reduce the candidates available as buyers. This is because there is a strong belief that placing the buyer's shares in the hands of the vendor (up to 50 per cent of total deal value typically) during the time of the earn-out closely aligns both parties' motivations, quite apart from avoiding the reduction in the amount of cash available for other growth-related purposes in the buyer's business. The painful lesson learned by those vendors who accepted Cordiant shares as part of their sale consideration is, however, a salutary reminder of the risks involved.

10

Briefing and managing the lawyers

THE VENDOR WILL HAVE BEEN ADVISED by the corporate finance adviser to select a legal adviser early in the sale process, ideally before it has formally begun, and to have kept them appraised of developments with the corporate finance adviser. Soon afterwards the corporate finance adviser should have helped ensure the company's ownership arrangements are appropriate and fully documented, and that there are no immediate and obvious issues likely to arise out of a buyer's due diligence review. Thereafter, the main focus of their initial involvement will be to reach the point at which a draft Heads of Agreement has been framed with the proposed buyer. This document, while not legally binding (save as to exclusivity and confidentiality – see below), is critical to the efficiency of the process, in that it should comprehensively and unambiguously set out all the key aspects of the agreement. This will in turn serve to brief both parties' lawyers as to exactly what agreements, conditions and protections they are requested to provide to their respective clients.

Heads of Agreement

A key objective for the vendor is to ensure that the Heads of Agreement represents a firm offer that is subject to a minimum of conditions. It would be normal, however, for the offer to be subject to receipt of full information, due diligence and contract, and it may also be subject to financing (often unavoidable unless the buyer already has available funds, because any third party investment that may be required is unlikely to be confirmed until signed Heads of Agreement are seen by the funders). If the offer is subject to finance, the prospective purchaser should be asked to provide evidence that such finance is available.

It is normal at this point for the prospective purchaser to be given a specified period of exclusivity, during which the vendor commits to refrain from talking to other parties. This is to protect the purchaser, who will now commit to external costs of due diligence, documentation, tax and other advice. The vendor will seek to restrict the exclusivity period to a minimum, as at this stage the objective is to close the deal at the agreed price and terms as quickly as possible. It is not unusual to have the period of exclusivity made subject to the buyer meeting specified timetable milestones. If these are not met, the right to exclusivity can lapse; this enables the vendors to get on with running their business if the sale does not proceed, and to return to negotiate offers from other interested parties.

it is normal for the prospective purchaser to be given a period of exclusivity

Contracts and agreements

Once the 'Heads' document is signed, a legal and accounting due diligence process can get under way. Meanwhile the buyer's lawyer will prepare an initial draft sale and purchase agreement for submission to the vendor's lawyers. At this stage the corporate finance adviser's lead role is taken over by the legal adviser. In our experience, however, it is vital for the corporate finance adviser to remain working in close support of the lawyer, as there are inevitably points of interpretation and understanding that require clarification from the original negotiations. Contract negotiations can sometimes lead to points of serious disagreement. These can prove insoluble between lawyers, and a delicate facilitation process is required between the parties. Given their interaction between the parties from the outset, the corporate finance partner is often best placed to take responsibility for this.

how and when the purchase price is to be paid is as important as the price itself

How and when the purchase price is to be paid is as important as the price itself. The buyer, in seeking to de-risk the deal and reduce its cost, will always want to extend the timing of payment as far as possible via the earn-out mechanism. The vendors will be seeking the same goals by maximising the proportion of the value to be paid upon closing.

Typically, a portion of the buyer's valuation is paid upon completion, say 50–60 per cent, in cash (or cash equivalents, such as loan notes) or shares. This payment is the money the buyer has at risk. If the business does not subsequently perform, the buyer stands to lose this investment. Accordingly, the buyer seeks to protect himself against this loss and the loss of further performance-related payments under the earn-out formula. The procedures the buyer adopts for this are usually the subject of much negotiation.

Like the buyer, the vendor also seeks protections. The main vehicles for both parties are:

Sale and purchase agreement

The buyer looks to this as the vehicle for setting out all the conditions applying to the definition of assets being acquired, and the means by which consideration is to be paid and when. Of particular concern are the subsequent payments, usually in relation to an earn-out, that are to be paid beyond the initial completion consideration. Ambiguity has to be avoided, given the considerable potential for misunderstanding over the conditions applying to such payments. One example of an issue requiring clarity is what happens if a shareholder leaves the company during the earn-out, and under what circumstances. Tax and accounting implications arise when deciding how to deal with this issue.

for the vendor, the most important protection is the guarantee of continued management control

For the vendor, the most important protection is the guarantee of continued management control during the earn-out period. This guarantee of management autonomy assures the vendor that the new owner will not interfere, second-guess or impose policies that will impair the vendor's ability to meet the minimum earn-out hurdles – or indeed maximise the value of the earn-out.

An extension of this issue is the need for agreement as to what management charges and other costs the buyer will apply to the vendors' company once it has been acquired. Agreement is also needed as to exactly what these relate to and what benefit will accrue. This is very important, as the charges impact on the profit of the target company and therefore the value to be achieved during the earn-out.

Service agreements and restrictive covenants

Another protection for the vendor that is usually provided is an employment contract that typically lasts as long as the earn-out. This assures the vendor that he will be given sufficient time to meet the earn-out goals. The buyer, in turn, will usually require the signature of the key personnel, not just the shareholders, on the service agreements. This will stipulate that if an executive leaves the agency, they will not work for clients or hire or work with key employees for a period of time. While it is good form to ensure that these are in place long before the sale process, the purchaser will invariably require new service agreements to be entered into. Other 'restrictive covenants' to be given by the key vendors will also be negotiated to limit the buyer's risks. Given that the buyer has no direct control over the goodwill acquired, at least during the earn-out, these risks are not inconsiderable. Such protections are often more restrictive than the covenants usually seen in service agreements – for example, setting out a time period during which the vendor is restricted from working for any competitive business in the same marketplace.

Warranties

These are assurances the vendor has to make about the substance of the assets being transferred. Examples are:

- That the financial statements provided by the vendors fairly and properly portray the company's true financial condition

- That there are no undisclosed impending or outstanding legal actions or other material, contingent liabilities

- That to the best of the vendor's knowledge, all the clients are satisfied with the vendor's services and accordingly would be expected to remain with the agency after it is sold

It must be recognised that purchasers normally attach great importance to the provision by the vendor of warranties covering the valuation of assets, completeness of recording of liabilities, and reliability of available profitability and cash-flow information. Moreover, they will expect such warranties to be supported by a material financial risk if they prove to be wrong. There will be a clear trade-off in terms of price and timing of payment of consideration on the one hand, and the willingness of the vendor to provide such assurances on the other.

an adviser will help the owners understand what is normal business practice

In this process, the vendors will be seeking to stick as closely as possible to the Heads of Agreement. They should, however, also anticipate the purchaser trying to justify a reduction of price or the introduction of more stringent terms and conditions, and be ready with a suitable answer. Should the due diligence process reveal discrepancies that would justifiably affect the valuation of the company, the vendors will need to be realistic in their response.

While it is understandable for the vendors to wish to limit as far as possible the extent of such warranties, there is a cost to this. Too much focus on this issue conveys a lack of confidence on the part of the vendors in their business. An adviser will help the owners understand what is normal business practice and try to strike a fair balance between value for the business and the risk of future claw-back. Aside from the threat of claims over vendor breaches of warranty, some purchasers also seek provisions to form part of the sale and purchase agreement. These determine to what extent the sale price may be retrospectively adjusted to compensate for unforeseen losses, costs or lack of profitability.

Disclosure letter

A common way of limiting exposure under warranties is for the vendor's lawyer (in close co-operation with the vendor) to produce a 'disclosure letter'. This is a document that sets out agreed exceptions to the warranties. Naturally, such disclosures need to be agreed with the buyer and need to be clear and understandable. This document can be very important in bringing together the twin strands of due diligence and warranties. In any event, the vendor's lawyer will seek to limit exposure under the warranties. Areas that may be covered include how long a buyer has to bring a claim, who can be sued, maximum exposure under a claim, and a level below which no claim can be pursued, even if there has been a warranty breach.

Tax indemnity

The buyer will naturally want an indemnity in respect of any undisclosed tax liabilities relating to the vendor's company. This indemnity will normally not be subject to any limitations and will generally last six or seven years, and could also cover interest and penalties that might be levied by the Inland Revenue.

Escrow funds

A portion of the agreed valuation (e.g. 10 per cent) may be placed in an escrow fund for a period of time (usually up to one year). This is the buyer's insurance fund, which enables them to recoup part of the purchase price after the closing if the vendor has fallen short with regard to the agreed-upon warranties and representations regarding their company.

Endgame

A common tactic of some purchasers is to make an abrupt and seemingly unwarranted change of position. This can happen at any stage of proceedings, and can seemingly throw the whole deal into jeopardy. It is particularly seen at the last minute when the vendors appear fully committed to the transaction. Should this happen, it is important for the vendors to keep cool and stick to their position. The strongest defence against this – subject to any right of exclusivity that has been granted – is maintaining an alternative candidate whose offer was not far from that of the preferred one and whose bid can be resuscitated.

One response to the tactic is to request confirmation that the purchaser is withdrawing their previous offer and therefore relinquishing their exclusivity rights. This threatened loss of exclusivity may bring the purchaser back to their senses.

11

Understanding the role of due diligence

IT IS CLEAR FROM THE ASHRIDGE STUDY that there is a need for a more efficient, rigorous and holistic approach to commercial due diligence, which must go beyond the standard financial and legal issues if it is to provide the buyer with a real perspective on the asset they are actually paying for – goodwill. In a post-Enron environment, in particular, the professional advisers involved have felt obliged to double and treble check everything they report on. This has greatly increased the cost to buyers (another influence on the preference for larger, uncomplicated deals), but has also greatly increased the burden on the vendor, and the evidence is that this is not always being well managed by the buyers.

post-Enron, professional advisers have felt obliged to double and treble check everything they report on

At this stage, with 'Heads' signed, the vendor will normally feel sufficiently confident that the deal is done to start to relax. That is a dangerous mistake, however, as the serious work is only just beginning. It is at this stage that very careful note should be taken of the sound advice being offered by the professional advisers, because an off-guard vendor can seriously affect their negotiating position by making ill-considered comment or action at what is a very sensitive time in the process – the due diligence and contract negotiation stage.

an off-guard vendor can seriously affect their position by making ill-considered comment

That said, it will generally be safe and proper to release more sensitive information and to allow the agreed candidate some access to the vendor's office. At this point, when there is a good prospect of a deal being done, it may be advisable to inform key employees, so that they become aware of and supportive of what is happening.

It remains a good tactic to keep certain positive information about trading in reserve. During the due diligence and documentation stages that follow, the vendor will be striving to avoid erosion of the price, or the introduction of onerous terms and warranties. Depending on progress in this, it is useful to be able to release good news that can enhance the negotiating position at key moments.

It is hugely important that care is taken to provide accurate information; that forecasts made are realistic and their basis understood by management; and that no material adverse information is withheld. In that event it is probable that any material discrepancies will be identified. Should due diligence reveal such discrepancies, the vendor will be in a weak position to resist an adverse effect on price and terms.

The kind of intangible factors to be interrogated in a more commercially-rounded due diligence – for both parties' benefit – include objective and qualitative assessments of:

- Market reputation
- Client relationships going forward
- Employee engagement (loyalty, motivation and advocacy)
- Supplier partnerships
- Cultural and commercial style and fit (parenting)

All of these are capable of being investigated independently and discreetly with a well thought-through commercial due diligence process, and in cooperation with the vendor. The last is particularly interesting and was cited by the Ashridge study as one of the critical success factors (CSFs) for successful acquisition. It is to be hoped, therefore, that this will more often feature much earlier in the courtship process (see Chapter 6) and not be left to this stage. That said, the commercial due diligence stage should in any case be seeking to verify the judgements made earlier.

12

Planning for post-acquisition communications, integration and motivation

THE FIRST DAY UNDER NEW OWNERSHIP is unquestionably the most important. It should start with a meeting of all available employees and an urgent plan to meet those who cannot be available at short notice. It is important to address the inevitable rumours head-on and treat people like intelligent adults by explaining in clear terms what the change of ownership means. It is reckless, in so doing, to raise expectations or make promises about the future that are unlikely to materialise, tempting as this may be in the spirit of comfort and reassurance that vendors will be seeking to offer.

there should always be a post-acquisition business plan

From the buyer's position it is important to see the acquired business as more than something which requires attendance at a monthly or quarterly meeting and the reading of additional regular financial reports. There should always be a post-acquisition business plan for the company, in both its stand-alone capacity and in the context of how the combined assets can be leveraged.

Communications

It is often left entirely to the management of the acquired business to deal with communications to employees, clients and the market. All too frequently they are given very little advice and support from the new parent, despite the fact that while they will normally never have experienced such circumstances, the buyer may have done so many times. Consequently, the subject gets little attention until the last minute because the acquisition process itself has been so demanding and preoccupying. The result is that it is usually inadequately thought through by inexperienced managers.

As the Ashridge research indicated, there is often a major disconnection between the principals and the staff at this time. The employees' perception is that they now have a new employer (and indeed new employment contracts are sometimes issued, just to underline the point). To them the previous employers are now 'rich', with different agendas associated with that understanding, and their new employer is remote and comparatively unknown. Ironically, their own importance is in fact now probably greater than it was before, as they are effectively part of the goodwill that has been sold. But this is not always appreciated or indeed easy to communicate, given that certain types of people may be inclined to use such an understanding to their advantage. In summary, these are delicate motivational issues for which good advice is not often made available, or indeed sought.

post-acquisition mismanagement is one of the important contributory issues for failed acquisitions

Another observed tendency is for the founder to compound the problem. Exhausted from the sale process, they will often slide away on an exotic holiday within a few weeks of the deal closing, with consequent risks to the business at a vulnerable time.

These may seem basic commonsense failings, but they are sadly still all too prevalent in our industry – serving to demonstrate, once again, how far it has to go to be considered as a mature and grown-up industry. Post-acquisition mismanagement is one of the important contributory issues for failed acquisitions raised in the Ashridge research.

Given these risks to impairment of value, it is extraordinary that more effort is not put into pre-planning. Almost always the deal becomes all-consuming, and completion becomes an end in itself, rather than actually only the start of the end – which will typically have at least three years to run before it can be judged to have been successful.

I have already indicated in Chapter 3 how success maps can be used to ensure an effective meeting of minds about what constitutes success. As well as identifying what success will look like, the maps delineate how it can be achieved and measured, including the all-important issues of business synergies, and communications to managers, staff, clients and suppliers.

Parent company intervention in the early days is often limited to accounting-style inductions into new reporting and cash management procedures required of the finance department and chief executive of the acquired company. This runs contrary to the vendor's expectation that their company will be of real interest to the buyer. In fact it can soon become quite demoralising for the company's management to realise they are actually simply another file in the

even modest attempts by the buyer to show a genuine interest in the acquired business can be hugely motivating

buyer's portfolio. By contrast, even modest attempts by the buyer to show a genuine interest in the acquired business – maybe even attempting to provide business opportunities – can be hugely motivating to the principals.

Obviously the best way to motivate managers is to allow them full responsibility to manage what, after all, they generally know more about than the acquirer. Of course, the earn-out concept encourages this, but entrepreneurs, like most humans, more than anything simply want to feel recognised and included. They will certainly expect at least some added value from the new parent, and where this is not forthcoming, it will almost certainly influence the relative lack of success of such acquisitions.

Integration

Integration of the acquired business takes two forms. If the company is to remain stand-alone, as is typically the case in a normal earn-out situation, then integration is limited to the issues of becoming a good member of the family. Aside from being fully versed with the procedures (largely financial) of the parent company, the main issue for the vendor is seeking circumstances which will assist them in achieving their earn-out. For some vendors, just being left alone to succeed without interference is regarded as a goal, but frankly this is a somewhat short-sighted view of the possibilities.

Every group will have potential business-building opportunities – access to clients and new skill sets, as well as more mundane but potentially beneficial opportunities for training and improved procurement of services, property, etc. However, these can remain elusive in some organisations, and this can partly be because of the earn-out 'ring-fence'. Really, though, it is up to the entrepreneurialism of vendors to seek out access to these opportunities. Potential business partners should be sought out among sister companies and the parent company badgered into providing introductions and support. To put it bluntly, those who don't ask won't get.

Integration obviously takes on a much more fundamental and complex meaning where the purpose of the acquisition is to physically merge with the buyer's own business. I am particularly indebted to Mike Walsh, CEO, Ogilvy & Mather, Europe, Middle East and Africa, for sharing with me some of his company's learning here. I have paraphrased some of the most important characteristics of successful integration programmes from those listed in their guidelines, as follows:

- Plan clear communications to all parties concerned. Integration is a task that cannot be just one person's responsibility. All parties involved should be briefed on their role in the process so they can properly anticipate the needs and time commitment for them and their staff.
- Implement assessment of human resource issues.
- Provide full induction into creative reviews, strategic brand and customer relationship management (CRM) processes. Translate and explain typical Ogilvy jargon, such as Brand Stewardship, Customer Ownership, Brand Print, etc.
- Be clear on reporting lines, and job specifications.
- Set agreed milestones to measure integration progress. Report on bottlenecks as soon as they are identified, and act quickly.
- Keep focusing on the key objectives for the merger: better solutions for our clients, and increased new business prospects.

There are a couple of additional guidelines for working with stand-alone acquisitions that are worth mentioning too:

- Help existing Ogilvy agencies to understand the disciplines and benefits of the acquired agency, and identify business opportunities of benefit to our clients.
- Protect the acquired agency from being swamped with requests for involvement. Initially they can be the 'flavour of the month'. Help to judge the seriousness of the requests, and focus on really major opportunities.

Motivation

Motivation of the vendors and their senior people is critical for a buyer. It is not unusual for a significant proportion (up to 40 per cent) of the initial valuation to be retained as part of the earn-out. This is in order for there to be a realistically accessible further payment at the end of the earn-out, although there are sometimes interim payments. Additional payments are available to reflect continued growth. All of this normally provides significant motivation for the beneficiaries of the earn-out, which can include non-shareholding senior managers (subject to some important taxation issues). Other senior people will need to be included in share options or other forms of incentive scheme.

One error to be avoided is the vendor thinking that discretionary staff bonus schemes paid prior to the sale can be stopped after the sale to bolster the value. Normally a buyer would not permit this, but if it were overlooked, it would be a serious mistake to think that people's expectancy of receiving bonuses can be crushed in this way. Key people will soon disappear in the face of such avaricious behaviour.

Indeed, some vendors are tempted to view each pound of expenditure as costing them £5, pre-tax, or more (dependent on the earn-out multiple) during the earn-out. This is another worry for buyers. But while prudent management of costs is always to be welcomed, risking client service or creative standards, for example, by restricting necessary recruitment or pay rises will cause the business to atrophy over time. Where this takes place in the last year or two of the earn-out the risk to the subsequent performance of the business can be disastrous.

Buyers often give a lot of attention to avoiding this. One approach is to provide strong profit sharing for the vendors and supporting management beyond the earn-out, and to structure the earn-out in various ways to mitigate the risk. Typically the earn-out will be at least based on the average performance over the period of the earn-out. Alternatively it may be based on the best two years, providing that no year is less than the base year. There are other variations on this theme.

These problems of post-acquisition communication, integration and motivation can be overcome with proper planning. No one wants an acquisition which leads to demotivation and loss of valuable staff, which does little or nothing for clients and fails to provide the forecasted returns to shareholders.

Consider Figure 10 overleaf.

High morale in an independent agency can take a serious dip when it is realised that new owners are 'in charge'. Misconceptions need to be allayed, and communication has to be constant, honest and positive so that people in the acquired company are nurtured carefully through into the new environment.

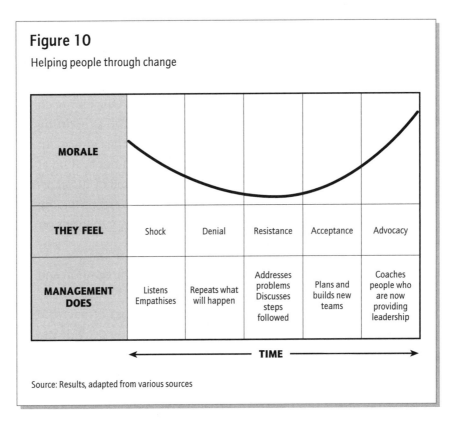

Figure 10

Helping people through change

MORALE					
THEY FEEL	Shock	Denial	Resistance	Acceptance	Advocacy
MANAGEMENT DOES	Listens Empathises	Repeats what will happen	Addresses problems Discusses steps followed	Plans and builds new teams	Coaches people who are now providing leadership

⟵———— **TIME** ————⟶

Source: Results, adapted from various sources

Achieving this is so much easier if a merger integration process is planned from the very outset. Such a process should have the foundations laid *before* the deal is signed. There should be an agreed business plan and strategy going forward and a vision for the agency that expresses its positioning, culture and structure, and addresses the important staff issues. There will need to be honesty, clarity and persistence during the courtship. If the acquisition is to result in a merger of two companies, then an integration team needs to be set up. It will be necessary to identify an integration manager, agree protocols of contact and establish a clear understanding of how the buyer's processes and style are to be communicated. The team's responsibilities will include setting out the vision for the new combined entity; for internal and external communications; for problem-busting and flagging up critical issues; and for exemplifying the benefits of change.

Rapid integration is crucial. This requires strong project management. Work processes and job descriptions will need to be revised or confirmed to ensure role clarity. There may be a need for individual discussions about new roles and responsibilities. There will have to be a strong staff focus on clients and work and explanation of the benefits of the merger to clients. The important thing is to treat people well. This includes giving practical help to leavers, in the form of career counselling and generous packages. There should also be skilled use of exit interviews.

It should never be forgotten that once the honeymoon excitement has died down there is an ongoing relationship. Accordingly, it is vital to have regular reviews of staff satisfaction, client satisfaction and retention, media coverage, mutual perceptions of external PR, contact protocols and processes, and, most importantly, the financial achievements as against the deal targets.

13

Dealing with the proceeds of the sale

WHEN YOU SELL YOUR BUSINESS you will probably own a combination of the following: loan notes, stock, stock options and cash, an earn-out that you are working hard to achieve, and a stock or loan note certificate somewhere in a pile of papers at home.

The first priority is to lock away the sum due for tax purposes so this is fully protected. No doubt there will be other personal expenditure for which you will have earmarked some of the proceeds. But beyond this there are opportunities to enhance or protect your wealth before crystallising the value of the non-cash elements, and this chapter raises some issues for you to consider. Let's look at them by asset class.

there are opportunities to enhance or protect your wealth before crystallising the value of the non-cash elements

Loan notes

Most loan notes are guaranteed by a bank and if required can be used to raise money. Banks will be comforted by the guarantee and it is not uncommon to see a loan-to-value ratio of over 80 per cent. It could also be 'cheap money'. If the loan note pays 0.5 per cent below bank base rates and you are charged 1.5 per cent over, the spread is only 2 per cent, and interest payments can often be deferred until the loan notes are redeemed and the borrowing repaid.

Where a company, rather than a bank, has backed the loan notes, the decision to lend against the notes will be determined by the underlying financial strength of the corporate issuer. In this case, loan-to-value rates are likely to drop towards 50 per cent or lower.

Stocks

The years after the stock market bubble burst in 2000 demonstrated how painful it can be to be locked into an equity position whilst prices tumble. But, in certain circumstances, you can buy protection (or 'hedge') against falling prices.

Here's how it works. You have a share that trades at £10 but you are worried about the price. You purchase an option that gives you the right to sell to a third party at £8, say, even if the price falls below £8. This ensures that you cannot lose more that £2. But you have paid for this right and it is often expensive. To recover some or all of this cost you do the opposite of buying the right to sell at £8 – you sell someone else the right to buy from you at, say, £13. The premium that you receive for this can offset the cost of buying the hedge.

You are now exposed to any price between £8 and £13; the rest is for someone else to worry about or enjoy. Boring maybe, but how many people do you know holding shares in some of the more beaten-up stocks in the sector, who are now wishing they had sought some sort of cover?

Is it easy to hedge? Not always, and a bank's ability to help will be greatly influenced by the following: the size and stability of the buyer; how actively the shares are traded; and the ease with which it would be able to unwind its position in the market. As a very rough guide, if the market capitalisation is below £500 million or if it is inactively traded, you may find yourself struggling. But it is always worth asking the question.

Once a position is hedged, it is easy to use the shares as collateral for any borrowing. A bank knows that its exposure is limited and may lend quite a high proportion of the value.

At the same time it may be possible simply to borrow against your shares, and many of the considerations that affect a decision on hedging will again come into play.

Vendors tend to borrow for two reasons. Either they want to raise funds for personal reasons, such as paying off the mortgage or moving house, or they want to diversify their risk in the markets. It is an unhealthy position to have all your wealth in the company that employs you and any adviser will tell you that a well-diversified portfolio reduces overall risks.

it is unhealthy to have all your wealth in the company that employs you

There are other more straightforward 'housekeeping' issues. Among these, we might mention holding your assets in a secure account, reserving for tax and using opportunities to defer CGT. Each should be evaluated against your current requirements.

Investment

When at last you can realise the investment – what do you do?

While it is impossible to speak for everyone in this position, people's needs tend to be remarkably consistent. They have fought hard to gain security, and the next thing they want is stability. They are looking for steady returns, not spectacular profits, and are particularly concerned about risk management. The important issue at this stage is selecting a well-recommended adviser, who should be able to develop an investment plan that reflects your needs, with a range of products and services to manage risk at their disposal.

You've sold the business, but you don't know what to do with your assets and may not know what to expect from the investment market. So take advice. Ask a private client institution to take you through the options available to you and allow yourself time to develop a long-term plan.

About Results

Results provides strategic and operational business consulting and corporate finance advice to the marketing communications industry. It focuses primarily on the creation and realisation of value for independent agencies.

Overview

- *Results* is a specialist consulting and corporate finance business, which works exclusively in the global marketing communications industry.

- *Results* provides a full range of performance improvement services (including business and operational strategy, client retention, and management development) as well as corporate development advice (including valuations, mergers, acquisitions and capital raising).

- The international arm of the practice, *Results International*, operates across more than 40 countries. Over 1000 marketing communication companies around the world have retained the services of *Results*. Some 140 sales and mergers have been managed by the practice.

The company has positioned itself as a leading authority on the marketing communications industry, and has adopted as its slogan,

A sense of direction in a world of change.

Acknowledgements

Many people have kindly contributed to the preparation of this book, offering valuable time for review, comment, and above all support. I have never attempted such a daunting task before (and doubt I ever will again), but the enormous sense of purpose I have received from colleagues, clients and many other friends engaged in the industry, who really did seem to share my sense that this book would meet a need, kept my resolve alive, despite moments of doubt. In alphabetical order, I feel particularly indebted to the following:

Roger Alexander, senior partner and head of the marketing services law group at Lewis Silkin Solicitors. He has thirty years' experience of deal making and acting for marketing services companies, public and private, UK and overseas and for leading figures in the industry.

Tim Birt, a solicitor specialising in corporate law, and the founder of Osborne Clarke's London office. Tim heads up its media and marketing services transactions practice, which specialises in assisting clients with complex and innovative issues and projects in these sectors.

Simon Hill, an MBA student at Ashridge Business School in 2002, who was sponsored by my company. We had met Simon a couple of years earlier when he was a shareholder and financial director at a leading PR firm. Previously Simon had been both an auditor and consultant at PricewaterhouseCoopers. The work carried out by Simon completely met our aspirations and we enjoyed participating with him on the research immensely. We are greatly indebted to him, as we are to his tutors and others at Ashridge Business School who supported him so cooperatively. Simon is now a partner in consulting firm Everymind, with whom we cooperate regularly on assignments within our industry.

Chris Jones, formerly chairman and CEO of J. Walter Thompson Worldwide. He is now a director of several companies including Results, where he is non-executive chairman. He also works as a management consultant and as an operating partner in a private equity firm.

Angela Lurssen, practice manager at Results, who relentlessly pressed on with the efficient organisation of the many facets of this book. Angela showed incredible tolerance and perseverance in the face of many frustrations and distractions, whilst still executing her 'day job' with her usual good humour and commitment. A real professional.

Mandy Merron, partner, Willott Kingston Smith. Willott Kingston Smith is part of Kingston Smith, one of the UK's top 20 accountancy firms. Based in London's West End, Willott Kingston Smith specialises in advising creative, communications and consulting businesses on all aspects of financial, fundraising, succession and business planning, as well as tax advice and pre-sale planning. The majority of clients are marketing services businesses which range from sizeable independents and multi-nationals to start-ups.

Noel Penrose, who worked as a chartered accountant with Price-waterhouseCoopers and has been involved in the marketing services industry for the past twenty years. Before joining Omnicom's Diversified Agency Services (DAS) division in January 1997, he was managing director of Ogden Entertainment in Europe, responsible for the management of sports and entertainment venues, sports rights negotiation and stadium financing and construction. He spent five years at Interbrand between 1988 and 1993 as group finance director in both London and New York. More recently he has moved back to Interbrand as CEO.

Mark Scott, an adviser to and investor in a number of professional service firms. Mark is a director of Ashridge Strategic Management Centre, where he conducts research into professional service firms. He was until 2002 a director of Lake Capital LLC, a large private equity fund focused on investing in people businesses, and he was formerly operations director at WPP Group plc, the marketing services group. He has had wide plc board level experience as a non executive director, including Watermark Group plc, Chime Communications Group plc, Fitch plc, and Chemistry Communications Group plc. He received his MBA from Harvard Business School and his BA from Oxford University. His widely acclaimed book *The Professional Service Firm, The Manager's Guide to Maximising Profit and Value* was published by John Wiley and Sons in 2001. He recently co-founded AIM-listed Cello Communications, a focused marketing communications group where he is CEO.

Lorna Tilbian, head of media research at Numis Securities, a rapidly growing investment banking and institutional stock-broking business, whose shares are quoted on the Alternative Investment Market of the London Stock Exchange. Lorna has provided outstanding investment analysis of the sector for many years, including six years at SG Warburg Securities and six years at Panmure Gordon, until joining Numis in 2001. She is a good friend to the industry, and, I'm delighted to say, of our small firm too.

Michael Walsh, CEO of Ogilvy & Mather, Europe, Africa and Middle East, whom I refer to in Chapter 12, and who so kindly provided me with a most instructive paper prepared by Wim van Melick setting out the company's learning about acquisitions, and their guidelines for integration.

Bob Willott, editor of *Marketing Services Financial Intelligence*. Bob has specialised in advising 'people businesses' for most of his working life. He is a special professor at the University of Nottingham Business School, writes regularly for *Campaign* and is a non-executive director of various companies, including Results.

Ashridge (www.ashridge.com)

Ashridge, one of the world's leading business schools, is an independent, not-for-profit organisation. Its combination of research, experience and practical application is currently making a difference to individuals and organisations in both the private and public sectors. Its activities include open and tailored executive education programmes, MBA, MSc & Diploma qualifications, organisation consulting, applied research and online learning.

Ashridge is consistently ranked as one of the world's top business schools in the annual *Financial Times* rankings. What makes Ashridge unique is its philosophy. It believes that all development must make a difference, be practical and be based on real issues. The majority of Ashridge's faculty have extensive international business experience, which they are able to bring to the everyday challenges faced by individuals and organizations.

Ashridge is accredited by the Association to Advance Collegiate Schools of Business (AACSB), the European Quality Improvement System (EQUIS) and the Association of MBAs (AMBA).

Last and not in alphabetical order, but by no means least, I have to give an enormous thank you to Sharon Studer, my personal partner, who really kept me focused on the mission and gave me terrific support, spending many, many hours poring over my manuscripts and finally helping me make some sense of it all.

Index